Lake Country

Lake Country

Kathleen Stocking

Ann Arbor

The University of Michigan Press

Copyright © by the University of Michigan 1994
All rights reserved
Published in the United States of America by
The University of Michigan Press
Manufactured in the United States of America
   Printed on acid-free paper

1997   1996   1995   1994   4   3   2   1

A CIP catalogue record for this book is available from the British Library.

Library of Congress Cataloging-in-Publication Data

Stocking, Kathleen, 1945–
   Lake country / Kathleen Stocking.
      p.   cm.
   ISBN 0-472-09516-1 (alk. paper) — ISBN 0-472-06516-5
   (pbk. : alk. paper)
      1. Michigan—Description and travel. 2. Stocking, Kathleen, 1945—
   Journeys—Michigan.   I. Title.
   F570.S76   1994
   917.7404'43—dc20   93-46406
                                                              CIP

This book is dedicated to my children

Let's go—much as that dog goes,
intently haphazard. The
Mexican light on a day that
"smells like autumn in Connecticut"
makes iris ripples on his
black gleaming fur—and that too
is as one would desire—a radiance
consorting with the dance.

—Denise Levertov, *Overland to the Islands,* 1958

Preface and Acknowledgments

All journeys are journeys out of the self, an attempt to get beyond what's known into something or someplace that will shift the perspective. The essays in *Lake Country* represent a series of journeys beyond my home in the far northwest corner of Michigan into other parts of the state. I wanted to understand myself in relation to something larger, or simply *farther*.

I had written a book about the Leelanau Peninsula, about the beauty of the people there and the beauty of the place. This book was well received but, as sometimes happens when one has said something that generates a greater reaction than one had anticipated, I began to question myself and my surroundings and so needed to get away, needed to be alone.

Michigan is a state where it seems one can travel almost indefinitely and never come to the end of the journey. This unlikely land mass, surrounded by water, hidden away in the center of the continent, has a three-thousand-mile coastline, uncounted dozens of offshore islands, fifteen hundred square miles of surface water on its inland lakes, and is a wild, forested, floating, watery world comparable to those of our most ancient legends, our most archetypal dreams.

Usually I traveled alone. On a few of the trips I was accompanied by my youngest daughter, Gaia. On others I took along one of our dogs. The most unlikely traveling companion I had was a small, brown field mouse who lived in the glove compartment.

I was drawn to islands. Some of the Michigan islands seemed among the last places in America to contain vestiges of the frontier of my grandparents and great-grandparents, and yet island life also seemed uniquely out of sync with any historical period. The island populations, like the characters in *Swiss Family Robinson* or the early Hawaiians, seemed as close to people being people—purely and unselfconsciously—as you could get in today's age or any age.

In my journeys I seemed to be searching for some essential truths. How should one live in this world? What is the thinking that drives this country? Those were the questions, unarticulated and inchoate for most of the time that I was traveling, that I see now in retrospect I carried with me.

If the Leelanau book had been perceived as being about the answers to how one should live in this world, then the Michigan book is about the questions. In the end what I found was something perhaps I'd known all along, and that is that, always, even in the worst moments, the unexpected kindness of human beings toward each other and the subtle beauty of nature sustained me.

The work for this series of essays was made possible in part by support from the following: a 1991 research grant from the Lester and Anne Biederman Foundation, the 1992 sponsorship of the Leelanau Children's Center, a 1993 individual Creative Artist award from the Arts Foundation of Michigan, and, currently, a three-year grant from the Michigan Council for Arts and Cultural Affairs to be writer-in-residence at St. Mary's School in Lake Leelanau.

I would like to thank my family, especially my children Jesse, Gaia, and Lilah and Lilah's husband, Bill Koski, for their sense of humor and caring throughout this work; I would also like to thank my mother, Eleanor Stocking, for her moral support. I am grateful, too, to my extended family on the Leelanau Peninsula, especially for the love and generosity of Duncan and Maggie Sprattmoran and their children Cody and Ramsey, who shared their home and their hearts with my youngest daughter while I traveled; Richard and Susan Och and their children Elizabeth and Shelagh who kept the dogs fed; Char Verschaeve and Bill Judd and their children Alita, Emily, Gaia, Justin, and Krya who replaced the hot water heater; neighbors Marcia and Tim Couturier and their children Smokey, Stormy, Tiffany, and Tricia who brought over food and other gifts; Freda Arrowood and her daughter Lark who provided many suppers and good times; Mike and Susan Lawler and their son Sawyer who listened; Mary Gadbaw, a registered nurse and friend, who provided emergency life-saving care when I became ill; Grant, Kyle, Steve, and Will Davis, as well as Addy, Emily, Erin, and Jordan Semer who supported the work; Grace Glynn who was always kind; Becky Thatcher who gave great Thai dinner parties, and countless others.

I wish to express my gratitude to the following: cover artist Jane Evershed for permission to use her image, *She Could Not Be Reached;* Traverse City graphic artist Laurie Davis who provided design suggestions to the University of Michigan Press; and illustrator Mary Harney for doing the series of black and white watercolors and pencil drawings in the book.

Writers and friends who helped by reading rough drafts were: Lu Capra, Jeanne Crampton, Cymbre Foster, Kathy Edahl, Judith Grossman, David Hacker, Susan Lawler, and Duncan Moran. My former teacher at the University of Michigan, New Hampshire poet Donald Hall, has been unfailingly generous with his letter writing, kindness, encouragement, professional guidance, and moral support throughout the twenty-five years I have known him. The University of Michigan Press's assistant director, Mary Erwin, was especially helpful, as were Christina Milton, Robin Moir, and several anonymous copy editors.

The librarians in the state who sent information, found information or retrieved things through interlibrary loan were indispensable to the work. Among these were Elaine Beardslee, Douglas Campbell, Katheryn A. Carrier, James Cavanaugh, Rochelle Hammontree, Dan Jamieson, Jane John, Carol Kuhn, Suzanne Latta, Marsha Meyer, Carolyn Russell, Joselyn Shraeder, Ann Sweeney, Marsha Thompson, Richard Waite, Patricia Wolters, and Marlas Wyckoff.

This long list and more besides, in all their variety, complexity and generosity, form the vital network of human beings who helped to make it possible for me to do this writing and I wish to acknowledge them here and say, "Thank you."

Contents

THE ROAD NORTH

The Moose in Negaunee

It must be after ten o'clock, but the air is still vaguely rosy-colored out, and as the last of the light fades, I am falling asleep in the low-ceilinged, upstairs, loft bedroom of a cottage on Mehl Lake near Negaunee.

The tepee-shaped room takes up the whole second floor of the dwelling, extending to the slanted eaves, like the inside of a child's homemade newspaper hat.

There are at least five empty beds around me in the dark. I can't see them, but I know they are there because I saw them before I turned off the light. At different times of the year the beds must be filled with cousins, aunts, uncles, grandchildren, but now there are only the spirits of these people here.

A row of square windows faces Mehl Lake. The windows crank out from old, tattered screens. Heat lightning zigzags from the dark sky above to the dark lake below. The plain of clouds in between is a low-vaulted chamber of fuzzy pink light—soft as moleskin to my touch or to my mind, if the mind can touch light—stretching for what I can only imagine is miles and miles over Mehl Lake.

The light in the room, like the light over the lake, seems gray-pink, and my bed seems to float in it like a boat.

Downstairs a white-haired woman I have just met sleeps on her sofa. She is Rose Collins, the grandmother of the young man my daughter Lilah plans to marry in almost exactly a year.

[3]

My German shepherd is curled up next to my bed, her head pillowed on my socks: my scent is her benchmark.

I wish it were so easy for me. I am trying to take my bearings from something larger, vaguer, to make sense out of the human existence I am part of as I fall asleep in this upstairs bedroom. The question for this evening seems to be: is the world made up of chaos or order? What has brought Lilah to Bill's family or him to her's? If the universe existed before thought, what does it all mean in the final analysis if there can ever be a final analysis in something with no beginning, and where does God fit in?

I'm falling asleep, picturing Lilah in this room; Lilah grown; Lilah womanly; Lilah beautiful. Then, Lilah being born. Lilah nursing for the first time, Lilah taking great drafts of milk with hilarious gusto, like Falstaff in a tavern. Lilah, a toddler—already characteristically self-possessed—looking at the bear clock in Central Park, head tilted to one side, watching.

Then Lilah's father taking her from the sitter and moving in with a student he loves somewhere in the city's vastness. My life becomes a New York nightmare where I know no one and my child is gone. I see myself standing in the precinct at 103d Street with its green-painted walls and fluorescent lights, a place as green as a grotto, as if I were looking through a banker's shade; I am trying to tell the police my daughter is missing, her father has taken her.

Through the bars that protect them from people like me who crowd their waiting room, they can't hear me; they can't help me. I am beside myself with grief as I rage through that dark city. "She is not herself," they say about me; or, "She is beside herself."

Then I wrest my child back and escape to a new life out in the country. In an old Michigan farmhouse, I am alone now with two children and penniless, my inheritance gone to the New York lawyers. Then, the camera moves: I see Lilah selling lemonade in front of our farmhouse at the dunes; Lilah swimming; Lilah getting all A's; Lilah in Switzerland, studying; Lilah making Phi Beta Kappa; Lilah preparing to be married to the young man whose grandmother has this cottage.

I had come "into camp," as Rose had called her place when I'd called from the pay phone outside the log cabin bar up on Highway 35 near Gwinn, in the almost-dark of a ten o'clock summer evening. I had driven down the sandy two-track through the pines, tired from traveling, glad to be coming "into camp" after crossing the interminable Seney Swamp.

My body feels heavy and I sag like a dolphin into the perfect indentation in the center of this perfect bed. I must be in Rose's bed. The indentation in the center would fit her body. She has given me her bed. Why? The question falls into my mind like something dropped into feathers. My body is heavy, but my mind is light. The question is too much for it and stays on the bottom like a sunken ship.

The cottage, what I can remember of it lying in bed, had shingles of a chalky, dusty green color. It was small, unpretentious, with a couple of propane tanks to one side and looked pretty much like every cottage from the 1940s on a lake somewhere in Michigan.

The most interesting thing I know of this side of Bill's family is about Olympia Bassetti, Rose's mother. The story is that Olympia Bassetti was a beautiful woman from a wealthy Italian family in Sestapoli, in the foothills of the Alps.

One version of how Olympia arrived in America is that her childhood sweetheart had left Italy for the iron mines of Negaunee, and she had followed five years later. Another version of this family myth was that she and her stepbrother had fallen in love back in Italy and Olympia had been sent—banished from the castle, is how I imagined it, like a princess in a fairy tale— with trunk loads of beautiful clothes to marry a miner in a rocky, sunless land across the ocean.

Negaunee. Gone. It even sounds like a place at the end of the earth. On the edge of gigantic and cold Lake Superior, in a rocky, barren place in godforsaken, wild, and uncivilized remotest North America, Olympia was forced to make a new life.

Nowhere could there have been a place farther removed from the flower gardens and festivals of Olympia's home in sunny Italy. Michigan's Upper Peninsula is still regarded as a frozen wasteland by many of those who don't live there. One University of Michigan commencement speaker, according to Bill, announced that there were *even* students graduating who had come there originally from the UP—as if the UP were a land more foreign and farther away than some unnamed island off Antarctica.

I asked Bill, when he graduated summa cum laude from U of M, if the people from the UP were given any special recognition at commencement, and he'd said, facetiously, "Yes, they had us all stand at the front of the stage so we wouldn't trip over each other." But, honestly, as a place in the mind's eye, the UP is far away from what most people can visualize; at the turn of the century when Bill's great-grandmother came there, it must have seemed like the far side of the moon.

Which story was the right one? Did Olympia Bassetti run away to her true love in America, or was she banished from the Sestapoli palace and gardens? Perhaps both versions were true, said my future son-in-law. Bill has studied law and logic. His mind could encompass two variations on a theme. My mind seeks one, something I can carry with me.

We all have to operate on the basis of what we think we know, but what do we ever know for sure? How do we connect to each other down through succeeding generations? Is there a reason a person meets one person and not another? Is it only in America that we have people from the four corners of the world marrying each other? These are the questions that float in this room of cousin ghosts I will never see.

Like a child, I get out of the bed and kneel beside it, hands folded like someone in a Christmas card. I say a prayer for Bill and Lilah, that they will be all right. I think the prayer will have a better chance of being heard if I say it in this way, in this place. I know I'm engaging in what is called "magical thinking," but I have to do something. I am not my dog and cannot be comforted by familiar scents, although I wish I could. It would be so easy then; I could sniff my way to all the knowledge I would ever need.

In the morning everything seems calm and clear. My mental perambulations of the night before have disappeared with the morning light. I lie in bed and wait to wake up, remembering the room; in my mind I am seeing it from above, piecing it together once more.

If I walked to the top of the stairs, I could look down and see half the dining room. In gray light I recall the way the stairs turn to the left halfway up; recall the old, unpainted floorboards, worn in the middle.

There is now enough light to see the other beds: two old metal ones, a spindle maple bed, an army cot, and the bed I'm in. There are the faded, wheat-colored wallpaper panels I now remember from the night before. I see Rose's robe hanging on a hook by the bed and see her shoes under the bed and know she has given me her bed. Why? Ultimate hospitality, I decide, with the clarity that 5 A.M. invariably brings.

I quietly slip down the stairs, past Rose sleeping on the long green sofa in her living room. I make myself a cup of coffee and sit down with the boxes of Negaunee and family history materials she has thoughtfully gathered for me. There is a big, cardboard box of family mementos: an article on her husband Sheldon Collins, an obituary for her father Pete Perucco, a photo of her beautiful mother, copies of the *KNEE-HI* news from Neguanee High School in the 1930s. I sort through endless old playbills, clipped articles, family photos. There is another big cardboard box on Negaunee history that includes many books and magazine articles on the history of iron mining. One pamphlet tells of how Chippewa guides led explorers to the outcroppings of iron ore. Then the miners came from Finland, Italy, Ireland, Scotland, Wales, Lithuania, Germany, England.

Not only are there many layers of indigenous and transplanted human cultures that have formed here over decades and even centuries, but the geology of the place, formed over eons, and the process of mining itself are wildly complicated.

Rose is up around me now making another pot of coffee. I

tell her I never knew iron ore was formed over billions of years by bacteria in the earth—which I still find hard to envision—and ask her if she understands the process of smelting or what a forge is, and she waves her hand in front of her face, as if waving away a mosquito. "Oh, no," she laughs, "but I could find you someone who does." But I am alarmed by this prospect. My mind conjures a mining and geology expert who will fill my mind with even greater quantities of technical and perhaps extraneous information.

We exchange pleasantries about dogs and weather. We are two women, separated by many years and many miles, now tenuously connected through my daughter and her grandson. She had baked raisin saffron bread, a Cornish delicacy, for my coming and now toasts two or three slices. The bread is delicious, the color of marigolds.

She suggests we visit her favorite place, an island in a marsh. I want to tell her about a whole mile-long meadow of grass with an ancient abandoned and weathered gazebo where I stopped three days earlier off U.S. 2, in a place that could have been Russia. There was a giant spruce. I sat under it with the dog. It was a day with a high, blue sky and air that smelled like soap or snow. The wind blew across this mile-long grassy plain with a sound like human breath.

Rose says we can walk to the place she calls "magic island" and this will give us a chance to walk our dogs. She has a tiny black-turning-gray poodle, Coco. And I have a big black and tan German shepherd, Crusher. Of the two, Coco is much more fierce and dominant. This amuses us, as Coco's whole head would fit in Crusher's mouth.

We walk first down the sandy two-track I had driven in on the night before, then to a meadow filled with sweet fern where the sun through the tall trees is making a lacy light. The sweet fern is abundant, lush, fragrant and smells a little like expensive Shalimar, but better.

I want to tell Rose about Lilah, how she was born so easily, how she always had an ability to hang on until she got what she wanted, but it is too soon, it is not the right time. It might never

be the right time. These are things we would talk about if there were enough days, if we lived across the road from each other.

Her taking me to the swamp reminds me of something my father might do, I tell her. He took visitors to exotic places in the woods and marshlands, the way a city person might take someone to an art museum. Rose and I are comfortable together out-of-doors, I think, as if we had known each other longer than we have.

I see small rare plants: the purple fringed orchid, Indian pipe, cardinal flower, and even rhododendron—past their blooming season. I am astonished to see rhododendron, which I have only seen before in the Catskill Mountains, and mention this to Rose. How did they get here? Did settlers bring them? And how could they survive the winters here? As far as I knew rhododendrons couldn't survive the winters in the Upper Peninsula.

"I have seen the most surprising things here," Rose says. "Plants we are told don't grow here, I have sometimes found in the woods and then never seen again."

On the way to Negaunee, Rose tells me the story of a place

near here on Highway 480, where the mining company was excavating, and they uncovered an ancient forest. The tops of the trees had been sheared off by what was believed to be the glacier. Here, scientists speculated, seeds of certain plants could have sprung back to life after eons. The rhododendron we saw that morning could have been planted by a settler, and somehow survived. More likely, that deep in the swamp, it was one of those rare species that survived this land's endless glaciations. It reemerged, part of another climate, another world, another time frame.

My mind drifts . . . Lilah's grandparents on her father's side, Sevek and Dorka, a stepbrother and stepsister who married each other, the only ones of their family to survive the Holocaust. Dorka had related how her brother had smuggled out a letter to her from the concentration camp. "*This is probably the last letter you will get from me,*" he had written. "I adored my brother," Dorka said in her inimitable and delightful Polish accent, "and that *was* the last letter I received from him." Lilah being born, coming out like a seal on a slide before the doctor arrived, "I'm here," her lungs open wide, and me thinking, *She's alive, she's getting air. She's alive.* We see beaver houses in the watery ditches on the way to Negaunee.

There is traffic on this highway, but just beyond the highway is the enormous Seney Swamp. I'd crossed through here the night before, terrified lest I should have a flat tire and be stranded there. Here are blue, crested kingfishers, pied-billed grebes, loons, red-winged blackbirds, muskrat, possum, dragonflies the size of clothespins and the color of pool table felt.

"My mother liked the woods," Rose says. "She liked to garden." I picture Olympia Bassetti, raised in luxury, with the freedom to wander and dream and read that would have accompanied that luxury, coming to the miners' shanty town, confined to a house, made to cook and clean and scrub instead of having it done for her. "She liked to sew," Rose goes on. "She did beautiful cutwork. Do you know what that is? It's a kind of handiwork, very elaborate. She didn't like housework. She kept a decent home, but it wasn't her favorite thing. I like the woods, too. I'm a dreamer. They say Italian people are that way."

In places along Highway 480 I can see parts of the Laurentian Plateau or Canadian Shield, that Precambrian rock that was made when the earth was first formed out of the void, the oldest rock, thrusting through to the surface here, a definite reminder of how indefinite humans are. We could go the way of the dinosaurs this afternoon, after lunch. We could become lunch, for alien creatures not yet imagined. *If fish could be our ancestors, what does the future hold?*

"We were very poor, but we didn't know it," Rose says. "Everyone else was in the same boat. We always had something to eat, even robins, which were delicious, with salt pork, a dry, dark meat. Winters were something. I can remember taking the rugs off the floor to cover ourselves at night."

On the horizon at the top of a rise is a strange structure. It looks dark and menacing, like a giant Darth Vader helmet. Rose says it's the top of a mine shaft.

"My mother came from Sesto Calende. She had hats with plumes, velvet suits, satin evening dresses. She made them into clothes for us children. She came to such poverty, poor dear. I often think of her. My mother was reserved. She loved to read poetry. She loved opera. She was educated by the nuns. Sesto Calende is in northern Italy. Her father owned a lot of land."

Negaunee sits directly on top of what was once one of the richest iron-ore deposits in the world, and when Rose was growing up in the twenties and the thirties, Negaunee was one of the wealthiest cities in the United States. Now it is one of the poorest.

Did other countries, other than America, have whole towns made and thrown away like Kleenex? Was this just an American phenomenon, this landscape littered with places that were once rich and thriving and now could barely be said to exist?

"We had everything in Negaunee," Rose says as we drive. "Opera. A symphony. A chocolate shop where we could get the most delicious chocolates. A Chinese laundry. We even had a Ku Klux Klan here, not that there were any black people, but these people hated Catholics. They used to burn crosses on the hill behind our house. We were scared to death."

Glaciers have rolled over this land at least four times, maybe more. During the last ice age there were a large number of giant mammals—elephant-sized hairy mammoths, bison, giant rodents, giant deer—present in the Great Lakes region. One of the great scientific mysteries is why these forms became extinct a few thousand years ago. There are some educated guesses as to why this occurred—climate change, no food—but no one knows for sure.

Up until the time the Europeans came there was still an abundance of smaller game here—bear, buffalo, moose, elk, deer, wolverines, bobcats, coyotes, wolves, caribou. Of these, only the deer remain in any number, although a few years ago the Department of Natural Resources did airlift moose in from Canada.

Rose says there are a few moose right in the city of Negaunee, in areas called "caving grounds," where it's unsafe for humans. Unsafe for humans means safer for moose. She says her sister-in-law saw a moose come right to the edge of her backyard. "The moose is a very shy, awkward animal," Rose says, "yet graceful. When it runs it seems to glide along in great strides."

I had read about moose, too, that morning, in the wee hours before even the birds were up. Moose are big animals. And, although vegetarian, they are very wild and seldom come near civilization except during mating season, when they seem to lack fear. One woman in Vermont who thought she'd look cute standing next to a moose in a picture, à la Walt Disney, got her comeuppance when the moose knocked her flat. She was lucky nothing worse happened. One bull moose in rut tried to copulate with a Volkswagen. Moose are seven feet tall at the shoulders and can eat a fifteen-foot tree by straddling it and walking it forward and then eating the tops.

Negaunee was built over mines, and where the timbers in the mines have rotted, Rose explains, the dangerous caving grounds have formed and the land is now unfit for people to walk or live.

Houses and stores have been torn down or abandoned and the land has reverted to grass and trees.

"Sometimes I wonder what they *did* when they excavated," Rose says. "We've lost our water. None of the water is fit to drink anymore. We have to pump it from Teal Lake and treat it. I can remember when I was growing up there were delicious freshwater springs everywhere. Now they're all dried up." This is the Negaunee version of the modern nightmare we are all horror-struck to realize is real: the loss of basic resources to sustain life.

The work in the mines was dirty and often wet. And, yes, it was dangerous. A shift was twelve hours and the pay was three dollars a shift. Many miners were injured, many were permanently crippled, and death was a daily risk. "The Barnes Hecker mine caved in in 1927," Rose says, "with the miners in it. It's just a burial ground. There's a stone up there. Over a hundred men died."

Rose's father, Pete Perucco, was lucky: he lived to be ninety-two. He was a timberman in the mines, which meant he built the supports for the tunnels. Rose says she and her two brothers, Eber and Lauro, used to bring their father his lunch at noon in the mine. "He'd come up with his iron ore-y clothes. I remember washing those. I miss the mine whistles. They'd whistle each shift." We are approaching Negaunee now and large outcroppings of rock show evidence of surface mining.

"All the captains in the mines were English," Rose says. "The Cornish. They knew their mining. And they were good managers. They made Cornish pasties, a kind of meat and potato pie. The pastie would sit on a tray on top of a bucket of tea; that kept the pastie warm. Or they would heat it up with a candle under a shovel, down in the mine."

"The Finnish people came," Rose goes on. "The men worked in the mines and the women worked the farms, but as soon as the men could afford to farm, too, they left the mines."

I know that Bill's family on his father's side is Finnish. Bill's Finnish grandmother Edna Koski grew up in the UP near the small town of Rock, a Finnish settlement. "In the winter,"

Edna had told me, when I'd visited her briefly before visiting Rose, "we'd come home [from school] in the dark—deep snows—we could hear the coyotes howling. My sister would say, 'I'm scared, are you?' I'd say, 'No.' I'd be crying. Then we'd see my father coming with the lamp. We could see it a long way off and it would move up and down."

Two years later Edna would delight a young New Yorker at a dinner party I would attend, by telling how she takes a sauna a couple of times a week and, in the winter, goes out and rolls naked in the snow. Edna is still beautiful, and not beyond enjoying shocking an urban young man or two with tales of rustic living.

Sandy flats terminate sharply against rock cliffs. Iron mines appear in the most unexpected places. Land forms change, seemingly without transition. I think of how the land reflects the way people who come there have often had to live also without transition—from one country to another, from one language to another, from one economic situation to another.

I think of all the different ethnic groups in the Upper Peninsula, all coming with their own language, their own customs, often creating communities as much like those back in the old world as possible. All of the groups, according to Rose, got along remarkably well considering their differences. And all now of those earlier generations, almost without exception, are watching sadly as their children move away to places where they can find work. "Our biggest export is our children," Bill's mother had said. Three generations, that's all it has taken, for their children to disappear into the melting pot.

"Most of the Italian people—our family didn't—made their fortune by bootlegging," Rose goes on. "My mother wasn't too well; the doctors performed a hysterectomy, and she was never the same after that; and when she would get sick, I used to stay with my uncle and my aunt would take care of me. They had a large room upstairs where they could take one wall down, and they had a still behind it: they made a lot of money. The trains would come in with grapes from California; wine was allowed for private use. They crushed the grapes with their feet, then later with machines."

Rose turns off the main road now and we wend our way back along a gravel road through low hills. Here are abandoned farms, unpainted and listing on the land. A mile further on, there are barren slopes, gravel pits, and boulder-strewn fields. Rose says that this is the area where she spent her childhood, in a mining settlement called Rolling Mill.

"I lived there," she says pointing to an old abandoned brown-shingled two-story home. "All the houses and gardens were on one side and all the mines were on the other." She names the families: Gilletis, Jacobettis, Flannerys, Chriis, Mainos.

She points to a brackish pond. "That's all filled in with water, but once it was mines. The mine shafts and buildings were all along this road. Now they're all gone. Miners used to bathe in what were called *dries*. There were troughs along this road that carried the runoff from the dries."

"Many of the Italian families had platforms built in their backyards for dancing on holidays. The Italians were very social. They celebrated every birth, every wedding, every occasion. They were a close-knit community. And there was everything here. A brick yard. Mining company offices. Stores. Homes. You can find old flowers, old foundations."

We go down a two-track behind a ravine where old apple trees have scattered their bounty in the grass. "There used to be *homes* here," Rose says, as if she herself has trouble believing it and so can't expect a stranger to these parts to find it credible. We get out and she bends and picks up a couple of apples. Moments later we're both gathering apples, our sweaters pulled up, turning us into marsupials.

I find my way around first one apple tree, and then another, and then another, until I have lost sight of Rose. She seems to be way down the hill. I lie back on the warm earth and feel my body thrum like a tuning fork.

Then I hear Rose calling my name, and in a moment we are back in the car.

We come to a railroad track and Rose pulls over and stops. She gets out and looks both ways, up and down the track. "There's no train coming," she says. She is standing now in the middle of the track.

It is a sunny day, but the sunlight is that thin, rose-colored sunlight of late afternoon, sunlight the color of white zinfandel. Rose bends to pick up something from the track. They are little pellets the size of marbles, the color of rabbit scat. She hands me some. "Souvenirs," she says. "Iron pellets. They fall off the [railroad] cars." She raises up from her bending and inhales the air, sighs. "It's funny, I don't feel a day older than when I used to play here. And do you know what? I miss the sounds. The trains. The mine whistles. Even some of the church bells."

We are driving back along a road that goes over a rocky hill. "Oh, look," Rose says, pointing to a house that looks as if it's being newly lived in, freshly painted. "This girl went away and worked in Chicago and is back living in her old family home. Let's see," she peers toward the yard. "Oh, look, she's got onions in her garden."

Now we are in Negaunee. There are many abandoned sections of the town that look like those places in Manhattan where whole blocks have been given over to weeds. Some are surrounded by chain-link fences with signs that say Keep Out or Danger, Caving Ground.

"There's where my husband's grocery store was," Rose says. "It was torn down. The building was leased from the mining company, so when the ground caved in under it the mining company bought my husband and his brother out—$17,000 for their business, $8,500 apiece. That's all they got for the work, thirty-eight years of their lives."

Here are whole streets of mansions, flush against wooded hills. A block or two of stores and then a block or two of idle land surrounded by chain-link fences. We drive down a beautiful treelined street that ends abruptly against an overgrown field and the stately maples and elms continue through the weeds and scrub brush as if no one had told them that the area of residential homes they once belonged to is no longer there.

Why did they build the town on top of the mines? Couldn't they have known they would cave in?

"I guess they didn't think about it," Rose says. "Maybe some of the mining was done after the town was built. At first they did surface mining—it was very unusual: the ore came right through the earth here to the top; you could see it—and then they went underground."

Still, it's unreal, a whole town built on a whim, caving in; as if the queen in *Alice in Wonderland* had decided to do a town instead of a party.

We pull into the driveway of a large home, a small mansion by today's standards. It takes me a moment to realize this is Rose's city house. That her cottage was her country house and this is her real house, or home. It has two and a half stories, thick walls, the kind of home that is cool in summer, warm in winter. There is a large portico, a garden out in back, and a garage that was once a carriage house.

We go up the steps into an oak-paneled foyer where French doors open into a living room with an oak-mantled fireplace. After a tour of the house—my favorite is the porch off an upstairs bedroom where it was never too hot and the maid could iron clothes in the summer—we return to the living room.

The plan is that I will spend the remainder of the day looking through more material relating to Negaunee history and then we will go out to dinner at a restaurant near Ishpeming, where the movie *Anatomy of a Murder* was filmed. The man who wrote the book for the movie, Robert Traver, aka, John Voelker, UP writer of note and fly-fisherman extraordinaire, had lived near here and only died recently, but somehow I can't get myself to care.

I sink into a large easy chair and start sifting through more articles. The sun is warm through the high, oak-framed windows. My mind is thinking about how Rose said the streets vibrated when the mining was in full swing, how in 1923, the movie theater on Saturday nights had a line that went around the block. How strange to think of all that now.

Diane Arbus's photographs from the 1960s show rich people

lying by their swimming pools in starkest sunlight, looking ghoulish despite their wealth. Her photos achieve a strange infrared reality that puts one off and at the same time draws one in, fascinates. I feel that way about Negaunee. There is no gradual transition from one land form to another, from one time frame to another, from the past culture created by mining wealth to the present one created by the abandonment of the mines.

The wild juxtapositions and overlapping time frames were especially striking while driving at fifty-five miles per hour down Highway 480, but are also an aspect of reality in Rolling Mill and in Negaunee itself, where a wooded hill sometimes penetrates to within a few feet of a commercial district and overgrown caving grounds are cheek by jowl with fancy homes.

It's like science fiction movies—twelve hours worth. The effect has been to make my mind feel whiplashed and overexcited.

Rose is moving papers around on her desk. I am watching dust motes in the shaft of sunlight crossing in front of my chair. The box of clippings sits beside my chair, barely touched, like food that is growing cold. My mind is going deil-a-dorc, dig-a-doo, deil-a-dorc, dig-a-doo, turning events over and over, like the clothes dryer tumbling one sock, one infant tennis shoe, one set of rompers with snaps, in the laundry room in the basement of our apartment building on Riverside Drive in 1972. Little logical Lilah marrying big logical Bill. Will their children have curly hair and broad shoulders like the people in the antique, gilt-framed photos on the wall behind me? When I visit them I can arrive in a hot air balloon, like Oz. Olympia Bassetti is beautiful in her pictures, softly beautiful with a certain sadness.

I am back in the swamp again, where the bright red spars of the cardinal flower float against the morning air. I am drifting over the Alpine meadows in Sesto Calende. I am Rose running through Rolling Mill. "Oh, look, she's got onions in her garden." The homely comfort of that. "Oh, look, she's got onions in her garden." I am cousins coming in from the beach at Mehl Lake, sand on my feet, going up the steps to the loft, peeling out of a wet bathing suit.

"I let you sleep," Rose says when I wake up much later in a colder room. "You seemed to need it." She has put a hot cup of coffee down on the table next to my chair. Behind me the high, oak-trimmed windows frame a gray and sunless sky.

We take a few minutes to gather up our things. We move outside and down the porch steps. The streets are empty, except for a few children playing. Somewhere someone is cooking pork roast and the scent wafts on the thin, cool evening air like a little invisible ribbon.

I look toward the end of the block where the same matching rows of trees—like the twelve spellbound dancing princesses of the fairy tale and the twelve spellbound dancing princes—are dancing across from each other on either side of the street, continuing on, block after block, finally disappearing on the other side of a chain-link fence, moving off into the scrub brush, apparently oblivious to the fact that well-kept lawns and houses and children playing have given way to tag alder and moose.

Morning Walk

There is a walk I take in the hills behind my house in the summer. Such a walk really begins before I begin it, because it begins in my mind before I am barely awake, with my mind picturing the walk; it begins slowly, subliminally, with that incredible bird chorus in the woods behind my bedroom that comes with those first subtle changes in light that only birds see, and it continues while I dress, drink coffee, and sleepily hear without hearing the sound of the crickets in the grass outside the open windows.

The first signs of dawn are shadows, shadows in the undulant grass, like the nap of velvet moved by an invisible hand, shadows where before there were none.

Outside, in the half light I can feel the dirt trail under my feet and smell the pines. I am moving unconsciously, without thought.

Out on Popp Road the asphalt heads up a steep grade for five hundred feet and then plateaus out, and then starts to climb again, doing this for a mile or more.

It has rained in the night and here crossing the road are dozens of wood snails. In the dim light they are almost invisible, wet and slick like the road itself, gray and so self-possessed—and all headed in the same direction—it is as if they are suited businessmen going to some convention by the pond.

I head up the hill, walking in almost total darkness, as the sun won't be up for another hour and this side of the hill is deeply wooded, dark and somnolent.

It is cool here, with that penetrating coolness that follows a night's rain. The birds are singing wildly, like a dozen symphonies, and with a jazzy exuberance.

Where the woods ends and the meadow begins is where I walk into the dawn's first dawning, that gray light that comes before the light of true dawn breaking.

In the very early morning the light is soft, filmy, mist tinged, tangible, sweet smelling, nourishing, and no wind blows.

A large deer grazes in a pasture. It stares at me for a moment, then lopes slowly into the woods.

Gradually the hills ahead of me are getting brighter. When I reach the topmost hill the sun comes up with a ringing in the air like a big brass gong.

I walk for miles in the 6 A.M. dawn—past falling-down farms, through old abandoned orchards, along the ridges of the dragon-backed hills above Lake Michigan.

As it gets warmer, I move back into the woods, taking the washout trail down a ravine to another field. This will bring me out again on this road, but in a different spot.

Deep in the woods I pass a familiar beech tree that has had the top broken off or rotted off for some time, yet two big limbs, like arms, remain half up-turned, Gumby-like, so the tree, with a big O-shaped knothole gaping at me, looks almost human. Here the wind in the trees is constant and soft, like water in a brook.

I move back down a lane that goes between two fields. The sky isn't more than pale blue yet.

Ahead of me I see moving, at the edge of a farmer's field, a red fox, bushy-tailed as any dream fox.

Back out on the blacktop of Linguar Road, there is no traffic. An old black and white collie with one leg missing comes out to the end of his driveway by the Popp farm and seems to say "hello," in his way. Then the Linguar farm with its blue Virgin Mary and the rows of blue Maxwell House coffee cans around the tomato plants.

The milkweeds along the road are in tight pods. Only the beautiful orange and black monarch butterflies eat the milkweed which is bitter as alum. Nothing, or nothing that I know of, will eat the monarchs because they are very bitter, even toxic, from eating the milkweed.

I like this walk at this time of day because I get to walk through several changes of light and temperature, the day and the dawn enveloping me by degrees.

I come to a patch of thick, cold fog near a spring fed marshy depression at the top of the hill. I am walking through fog so dense I can barely see the outlines of trees at the edge of the road.

I first hear and then see—a great huge bird take off from a high tree—loud as a horse if a horse had wings. This sound will stay with me for days, years, and I will puzzle over what bird it was. It will become a dream image, an atavistic archetype from my primitive past, my primitive present.

By the time I reach our small village, the place is waking up. Wayne Plamondon at the grocery store is putting the newspapers out. He's dragging his display of charcoal briquettes to the place near the blue pay telephone. He's watering his flats of pink and purple petunias.

I get my mail at the post office and walk home along the highway, along M-204. The sun has burned off the last of the morning mist and no prehistoric birds fly from tree tops.

Cars pass. There is dust now. I turn in at the two-track to my old house, up past the hot smell of the pines, the cascading slopes of pine pollen. My morning walk is over, my workaday day has begun.

Drummond Island

This is a story about an island, the people who live there, the day corporate development came to town and the day it left. It is a story about Drummond Island, an island in northern Lake Huron at the mouth of the St. Marys River, where in 1985 Domino's Pizza magnate, Tom Monaghan, began creating a corporate retreat. It is a story about the newspaper, the *Beacon Journal,* that was born out of the controversy. It is a story about change, stasis, pioneer values, and democracy.

Drummond Island, known throughout the Great Lakes as "hospitality island," was first homesteaded in the 1850s, and in many ways life there, even recently, resembled that of early pioneers. "People could hunt, fish, grow their own food, and children didn't have to be dressed up to snuff," commented island historian Katherine Lowe. Those who stayed on the island often married each other and over the years became inter-related, an extended family.

"We look out for each other," said Denny Bailey, owner of Yacht Haven and a descendant of the first woman on the island, Betsy Seaman, who came here in 1853. "You grow up together, you take care of your own. No one starves. If there's a kid at Christmas [without family or without presents], we make sure that child's taken care of. If a house burns down, we have a bingo or something."

I visited Drummond Island first in the late fall of 1989, right before deer-hunting gun season. It was already dark when I got on the ferry at De Tour to cross over to Drummond. From the mainland at night, Drummond looked like a wedding cake, all lit up, like a fancy Greek island where rich people stayed. I thought all the lights I saw toward the west end of the island must be from a big hotel, like the Grand Hotel on Mackinac. But when I got off the island and turned that way, I discovered a dead end and KEEP OUT signs.

Slowly I drove back the other way. In the light from a full moon I could see that next to the road I was on ran a larger, wider, boulevardlike road lined with boulders. It looked like it must go to a castle. Perhaps it went to the place I'd seen from the ferry.

The next day I learned that was the road that went to the dolomite quarry and it was so big and wide for the quarry trucks. All those lights, which had looked so inviting at night, turned out to be the yard lights of a very bleak and uninteresting quarry complex. Even the mining of dolomite, so I was told by Gib Aikey, the man in charge, was a petered out enterprise, not the booming industry it had once been.

I drove then that first night to the Northwood Bar and Restaurant, owned by Denny Bailey's parents. Here was the island hangout of local people and blue-collar hunters up from Flint, Pontiac, and Detroit. "When you earn your livelihood from tourism," Denny Bailey said, "you learn that if you make somebody happy, they want to come back."

The Baileys, the Seamans, and the Mosers have been on Drummond since the 1850s. "When I grew up I had four sisters. We all went away to college," Denny Bailey said, "but I had no desire other than to come back here and take over my mom and dad's business. I love to hunt, I love to fish—it sure beats city life—and it's home. It's where I was born."

The island, rich in deer, bobcat, and bear, is beautiful in its own rugged, untouched way. With its many bays and inlets, rocky shoals, and the good-sized Potagannissing River, it has excellent fishing. The 87,000 acre island is the third largest freshwater island in the world. For those who love hunting and fishing and the clear and comforting familiarity of a small community, it is a kind of earthly paradise.

But it's not necessarily a life everyone would love. "Island life is claustrophobic," said Gib Aikey, the John Wayne–style Texan who managed the dolomite quarry, "everything revolves around that ferry." Aikey, who was working twelve hours a day, six days a week, said, "On Sunday we go to the Soo [Sault Ste. Marie], have pizza. Other than that, readin' a book, or restin' on the couch." Aikey said he couldn't wait to leave every year on the last day of November and go home to Texas for four months.

But Tom Monaghan, in an article in *Michigan Living* in 1987, said it was the beauty of the island and the beauty of its people that he fell in love with when he sailed into Potagannissing Bay in the fall of 1985. Monaghan had the money and the drive to bring about big changes on Drummond. Among other things, he expanded the island's airport, built an eighteen-hole golf course, and reportedly poured more than fifteen million dollars into his twenty-five hundred acre public lodge and retreat on the island.

Robert Conard, owner of the Drummond Island Cabin Maintenance Service, said it was the very things that Monaghan loved about the island that his corporate development threatened to destroy. Conard launched a monthly newspaper called the *Beacon Journal,* he said, to "awaken the moral force of the citizens." He said he didn't want the multimillion-dollar development to "destroy the unique island flavor that sets apart remote cultures from the seemingly endless array of stupidities that mark contemporary cultures everywhere."

Conard and Monaghan were initially the central characters in this contemporary drama of cultural change. Conard was the self-educated intellectual who perceived the threat big-time development might make to this island culture and so became a one-man newspaper. In the tradition of colonial pamphleteers Tom Paine and Ben Franklin, he took it upon himself to delineate the issues for his fellow islanders. Monaghan was the self-made millionaire who has said he grew up in poverty in Michigan, a man who started out as a pizza delivery boy and eventually created the multimillion dollar Domino's Pizza empire, a bold and vigorous entrepreneur right out of the pages of a Horatio Alger novel. Conard, from his rustic Drummond home on Sheep Ranch Road, where a kerosene lamp provided the light in the absence of electricity, observed at one point in the controversy, "A culture is literally dying here."

Conard came to the island in 1974, after years of studying philosophy and literature and more years of traveling. He married Margeanne, a young widow and mother of two small boys. Margeanne had recently lost not only her husband, to a car accident, but her kindergarten-aged daughter had been run over by a school bus. "How did you survive?" I asked Margeanne. "I wouldn't have without Bob," she answered quietly.

Conard fell in love with both Margeanne and Drummond Island and settled down to hunt, fish, and, he explained, "simply *live*" in what he saw as one of the last traditional village cultures in America. "You know, coming here from the city, and seeing these people here, people of tremendous character, it's like there's a natural perfection. And the island itself is just so beautiful. I'm a fanatic walleye fisherman, so when Domino's began pumping effluent into the bay from their sewage system, I guess I felt strongly that I had to do something."

The next day, Conard was driving me around in his pickup truck, showing me the island as he first saw it. "This is the Bailey family complex," he said, as we drove down a rocky, shore road. "They're all gathering for deer camp."

It was November, sleet season. Alternately it rained and snowed and then the sun would break through, shining on black and blue water, brown woods with a thick carpet of leaves. We drove finally on a deeply rutted, narrow road through a dense wood. We came to what looked like German guardhouses in the Black Forest. They were tall, narrow, dark, and looked like the kind of things that toy soldiers come in at Christmas.

I turned and looked at Conard, "Guardhouses?"

He laughed, nodded his head. "This is the road to the Domino's Lodge. That's the kind of thing they do. It just makes no sense." Farther on we came to elaborate, and presumably, very expensive log homes that were part of the Domino complex.

Conard drove down a street of ordinary, well-built homes. "There's the house of a good building contractor, one of the most affluent guys on the island," he said, pointing to a solid but unpretentious home, and then, pointing to the house next to it, he said, "And there's the house of one of the guys who works for him—right next to it. You can't tell the people who have money here, from the people who don't. That's an amazing thing today. There's really no class system."

Conard took a two-track back into the woods. "That's where my friend, Pete Cross, lives," he said, indicating a standing chimney next to what looked like a dump. "Pete lives at the dump," Conard said, obviously enjoying the shock value of this. "Pete's also good friends with the island historian, Katherine Lowe. He lives there." He pointed to a square, green trailer. "He's an artist." I told Conard I'd now heard of three artists who lived near dumps. "Materials," he said, then he adds, "Pete did the illustrations for the *Beacon Journal*."

"It wasn't that many years ago," Conard said, "when it was very tight. There was an expression, 'There was never a Depression on Drummond,' and that's because there was always a Depression on Drummond. So you have all this independence, this rural character, but you also have people who are so independent they don't have a zoning code. And you still have the thing of people here who, when Monaghan came with jobs, were just so glad not to have to do that grinding physical work anymore."

We ended up coming down to a small village on the rocky shore of the island. This was the original village, Conard said, and is called simply "the settlement." There's an old post office, an old general store. I had been there the year before and a lady who worked in the store had loaned me a needle and thread—*her* needle and thread, that she'd had to run home to get.

The general store was like the ones I used to see in small towns in rural Vermont in the 1970s: a three-story, white frame building with a porch running across the front of it, cement steps you could sit on, a sign in the window that said, "Night Crawlers," and at one end of the porch, one of those old-fashioned, faded-red, chest-high Coke coolers—the kind I remembered from my childhood, where you reached down into melting ice water to get your pop. We could have been somewhere in Mexico, I found myself thinking, if it hadn't been snowing.

"My main objection to the development," Conard said as we returned to his pickup truck after a brief stop at the store, "is sociological, the change in the community. For me, moving here, the thing was to live in a traditional community. There's very few of them left anymore, and to watch the changes, it's really shocking."

Down near the water he showed me a small park with a large, plain-looking, gray-brown rock in it. Conard said a brass plaque on the rock commemorated Betsy Seaman and the eleven children she raised alone after her husband died. Betsy Seaman is a Drummond legend. One story told of how the dauntless Betsy loaded a calf onto a "jumper" sled, took it and two small children across the ice in winter to a Canadian dentist, sold the calf to pay the dental bill, and made the trek back to Drummond again; this was reportedly a dangerous journey where the uncharted ice and the snow had prevented many men from making the trip.

These were New Englanders venturing into the Michigan frontier: the family names of Drummond Island's original settlers were those one sees on tombstones in Connecticut and Massachusetts: Baileys, Butterfields, Fairchilds, Pierces, Mosers, and Churches. John T. Nevill writes of Bailey scion George Warren Bailey, "He was as 'down-east' as the Boston Commons . . . when he spoke, it was with the characteristically broad vowels of old Boston."

The communities these intrepid pioneers established in the Midwest were not very different from those Back East, and on the Lake Michigan islands and other pockets of "unchange," they continued in close to their original form right up until almost the present day. Those early East Coast settlers launched themselves and their offspring with all the fortitude and zeal of the first pilgrims at Plymouth Rock.

Back in Concord, right about the time Betsy Seaman was making her home on Drummond, Henry Thoreau wrote, "To Americans I hardly need to say, *Westward, the star of empire takes its way*. As a true patriot, I should be ashamed to think that Adam in paradise was more favorably situated on the whole than the backwoodsmen of this country. Our sympathies in Massachusetts are not confined to New England; though we may be estranged from the South, we sympathize with the West. *There* is the home of the younger sons, as among the Scandinavians they took to the sea for their inheritance."

"The local people are here because they were born here and they love it," Conard said as he offered his interpretation of events. "It's a traditional village culture. When Domino's came in, it started to change. People felt it and I just kept hoping people would say publicly what they were saying privately, but there was the matter of jobs. A lot of people who spoke very strongly against Domino's changed the minute a member of their family or a relative went to work for them."

Drummond has a town board, Conard said, but "the people on the town board are, traditionally, governing families, so if you say anything against anything, then it comes down to, 'Well, were you *born* here?'"

Conard wasn't born there. In that way he and Monaghan are alike; in their love of the island, the two men are alike, too. Ironically, although they represent different ends of the spectrum in terms of their ideas about what's good for the island, the two men are also alike in bringing the twentieth century to the island. Conard's ideas about the environment, his intellectual sophistication, and his awareness of American pioneer values make him as much of a modern phenomenon on Drummond Island as Monaghan's private planes, corporate money, large scale development, city-style log cabins, and Black Forest guardhouses. So although both men have diametrically different views on development and preservation, they both represent incursions of the modern into this relative outpost.

Conard said he was concerned about the changes Domino's would bring from the moment it arrived. "But what fired me up," he said, "was when they were going to dredge Maxton Bay so Monaghan could bring his boat in there. Maxton Bay is perch spawning grounds. It seems so profoundly stupid, just insane, to ruin the fishery."

Monaghan, who has said he considered Drummond Island his second home and spent about a weekend a month there, said in the *Drummond Island Digest,* "I have a great desire that everything I build here blend in with the surroundings."

A boyish, friendly man, an ardent Catholic, Monaghan said at a town meeting, "For good or bad, things can't go back the way they were. If we tore Domino's Lodge down to the ground Drummond Island would never be the same. Everybody in Michigan knows where Drummond is now. It will prosper with or without us."

People had seen maps drawn up that had the offshore Graveyard Island Monaghan owned, renamed Domino Island. Rhinehart Lake on the Domino property was renamed Lake Marge, after Monaghan's wife. People had visions of the island becoming a pizza Disneyland with names like Anchovy Alley replacing roads named for islanders.

One of the most controversial things Monaghan did on the island was to throw a Halloween party in 1987 that was quickly dubbed "wretched excess" by newspaper pundits. He gave away thousands of dollars worth of goods to party-goers and planned an Indian powwow that included a midnight foray to the former Graveyard Island where Native Americans from Sault Ste. Marie were to dance on the graves of their ancestors for the entertainment of assembled guests.

"But the God of Taste was awake that night," Conard commented wryly, "and the water was too rough for them to cross to the island." Richard Brunvand, Domino's public relations representative, when asked if Monaghan didn't think such expenditures and activities might offend some people said, "I'm sure none of that went through Tom's mind when he did it. You have to understand the kind of guy he is; for him it was just a matter of really celebrating the Tigers's victory and being very good to his friends."

And the locals were inclined to be tolerant. When asked about the "wretched excess," ferryboat captain Fred Moser said, "It's his money. I guess if he were hurting someone or hurting the island, I'd mind. As it is, I don't care at all."

Moser, who was speaking in the kitchen of his ranch-style home while his wife baked cookies on one side of the room and he cut up a deer [killed during bow season] on the other, added, "I think the quality of life here is better than it is in the cities. People here care about each other." Then he said, "Monaghan will change the quality of life here, and not necessarily for the worse." Moser said his children would be able to stay and work on the island now, something they wouldn't have been able to do before.

Monaghan had come under fire from some quarters for chaotic management at his lodge, for low wages, random layoffs, and for not buying locally and using local contractors. "Denny Bailey's the only one still workin' for 'em. Denny understands rich people, how to work for 'em," commented cement contractor Pat Kelly, a burly Vietnam veteran whose great-great-grandparents homesteaded on Drummond. Kelly added that he thought Tom Monaghan was a fair, just, and honest man.

"I was out there pouring cement on a Saturday," Pat Kelly said. "My men were off, and Tom jumps across this ditch I'd just poured—you can't call him Mr. Monaghan, he corrects you—and he holds out his hand and says, 'How they treating you, Pat? What do you think of our project here?' He always says that, 'How they treatin' you?' I guess I should've told him what I thought (about not getting cement contracts) right then, but I didn't want to rain on his parade. He's just so high on Drummond." "I think the downstate press has been unfair to Monaghan," Kelly reflected. "People on the island are for him. I don't care if I never get another contract. I'm for him."

Monaghan's development style on the island had been fast-paced, flamboyant, enthusiastic, and often lacking in planning. It was the latter that Conard had objected to. He said Domino's built the sewage treatment plant and began releasing the effluent into Potagannissing Bay, without doing an environmental impact study. After the fact, Domino's spokesmen said the effluent was cleaner than the water in the bay. Conard maintained that the effluent was warmer than the bay water, and that the bay is too shallow for it, and that the walleye spawning grounds were put at risk. This, like many other environmental issues, would be difficult to prove without extensive study.

Conard drove by the golf course Domino's put in. He pointed to the homes of people who lived around the golf course. "Their well went dry," he said. "Those people on the other side of the road, their well went dry. Of course it was a dry summer. But then you have the chemical runoff from the golf course to contend with, too. It's very toxic. It goes into the surface water. It goes into the groundwater."

Conard said that when the Domino's golf course was built and they began pumping thousands of gallons a day out of the island's shallow aquifer, several wells around the golf course went dry or lost pressure. Domino's spokesman Tom Minick responded that drought and other considerations may have affected the wells. Conard maintained they should have been pumping out of Potagannissing Bay, with its unlimited water supply, from the beginning.

Journalists from all over Michigan were fascinated by the idea of Domino's money coming to this relatively unknown Lake Huron island and by Conard's role as the island's one-man newspaper. "People who've written about it boil it down to the lowest common denominator," Conard said, "and that is: does Monaghan have a right to be here? That's not the question. He *is* here. The question is, does he have a right to degrade the environment because he provides a few jobs? I don't think he does. I just don't think he does."

Listening to Conard, it was hard for me to follow all the issues. They seemed complex, controversial. And Conard said he himself had a hard time staying on top of the issues. He said each time he had an environmental question, it took "immense amounts of time and money" to do the research. He had to make long-distance phone calls, send for written material, then double-check and triple-check and cross-reference his information. "Subject for subject," he said, "It was a full-time job just unravelling the bullshit." We stopped for lunch at a rustic bar: Chuck's Place. Here everyone seemed to know Conard. Owner Chuck Moser, one of the many Drummond Island Mosers, is a big, friendly, red-headed man. We got to talking. I learned Chuck is a relative of a neighbor of mine on the Leelanau Peninsula. Small world.

I also learned that Chuck and I had had similar experiences growing up in the rural Michigan backwaters of the 1950s. His years growing up on Drummond Island, his going away and eventual return, mirrored that of myself and many of my schoolmates on the Leelanau Peninsula. The jobs and schools had been different, but the desire to leave and then the desire to return had been the same. Chuck Moser had gone to high school off the island, in De Tour, taking a two-hour bus ride and ferry ride each day. He had spent two years going to college in nearby Sault Ste. Marie then he had quit and had gone sailing for a year on a Great Lakes steamer. Then he had worked in a drop forge in Lansing for a couple of years, producing parts for the auto industry, heating steel in 100 degree heat, winter and summer; then he had returned to the island where he'd worked odd jobs, cut firewood, and had drawn unemployment until he got work with Reed's Sawmill driving the forklift; then he had gone to work bartending at the Northwood for two years, then he had gone to work for the dolomite quarry for four years loading ore boats, by which time he had saved enough money to open his own place.

There's little crime on the island, both Conard and Moser agreed, because any robber would be caught before he got to the ferry. And there were few fist fights on the island or even feuds. "You're forced to be tolerant," Conard said, "The levels of tolerance are endlessly fascinating. You can be mad at someone, but you're not allowed to be mad too long. With an island, you can't get out; the best you can do is go in a circle."

Over french fries and hamburgs, Conard spoke at length

about the impact of the large-scale Domino development on the fragile island ecology. "Common sense," he said, "tells you this island is not going to handle this size development." He gave example after example of development methods that he thought had caused potential environmental damage, when a nondamaging alternative was available.

He admitted that his charges of environmental damage—for instance, those about the temperature of the effluent from the sewage system hurting the fishery, or the allegation that the constant watering of the golf course was causing the island's shallow aquifer to be depleted—would have been difficult to prove without independent environmental impact studies. These were studies that would have had to have been funded by the state or the township, and that Conard alone could not conceivably conduct or finance.

After bankrupting his family savings and straining his marriage to the breaking point, he had finally decided to stop publishing the *Beacon Journal* in the fall of 1989 with a "Swan Song" edition. In an editorial published in September, shortly before I had visited, Conard had written: "As all things begin, so they must end . . . we are putting out the lights at the *Beacon Journal* with this final edition.

"The thrust of the paper was to accomplish two things: one, to awaken the moral force of the citizens that they might stand up and insist on responsible behavior from the developers. It was our hope that this zeal, the result of everyone's love for their island, would take the form of standing up at town board meetings, writing letters to various editors of various publications; that, armed with a delineation of the issues by the *Beacon Journal,* these same people would of a body insist to the town board, the Michigan Department of Natural Resources, and Domino's, that 'jobs-only' was not enough. It was our hope that all citizens would speak up for the physical integrity of their home."

"Bob was a crusader," said Ann Stadler who used to put out the *Drummond Island Digest,* an upbeat monthly created in response to the *Beacon Journal* and funded and edited by the Domino's public relations department. I spoke to Stadler a couple of times and to Monaghan's public relations man Dick Brunvand several times, but Monaghan stayed out of the limelight, and I never got a chance to talk to him.

Most of the local people commented diplomatically about both men and complimented both Conard's contributions and Monaghan's contributions to the island. Monaghan's views in favor of development and Conard's against were fairly well known by the winter of 1990, and most of the island's longtime residents were preferring to stay out of the controversy.

At the J and R Restaurant, one of the construction workers I had talked to over coffee, the week before deer-hunting season, praised Conard for "bird-dogging 'em pretty good on these issues." Another man in heavy work clothes credited Monaghan for bringing jobs to the Island. Up at The Four Corners, Ruth Klamerus, owner of Sune's Home Center and Hardware Store, said, "What Domino's has done for us is create year-round business, create jobs, which creates money and improves the economy."

Conard was praised, even by people at Domino's, for his intelligence and knowledge of environmental issues. "I was impressed by him," said Tom Minick, director of Domino's operations on Drummond. "He made us think," said public relations man, Dick Brunvand. But both men criticized Conard for having a "one-issue" newspaper.

And Conard said he didn't want Monaghan's corporate development to leave the island. He had said all along that he approved of the Domino's employee incentive program at the Lodge and would have liked to see Monaghan implement the scholarships for local youngsters that he talked about during early stages of the development.

"We were successful in preventing the dredging of Maxton Bay," Conard said, "and we prevented Domino's bank from coming to the island. If you have a community of 700 people and you're the largest employer and you own the bank, you have enormous power. If you have a well going dry, for instance, and a loan at the bank, how much are you going to complain?" (Public opposition to the dredging mounted during one summer, but Domino's officials said the plans were scuttled because the state would have only permitted a one-time dredging. The bay would have had to have been dredged annually for the boat to come in and out, they said.)

After I left Conard that fall day, driving south through a swarm of hunters going north for the annual hunting ritual, I imagined that Conard would retreat to his own life and Domino's would play a larger and larger part in the resort business of the island. Conard talked of "moving on" and I thought he might.

But in the summer of 1991 I made it back to Drummond and I ran into Conard in Sune's Hardware at the Four Corners. He said he and Margeanne would be home later that evening and invited me to stop by.

I wended my way along the island's shore road, past the Northwood Restaurant, past the Settlement, past Chuck's Place, to Sheep Ranch Road. I didn't know why it was called that because I didn't see any sheep, although I did see deer. I also saw a whippoorwill and heard it call, something I hadn't heard since my childhood. Conard still had no electricity where he lives. At his place there's an old weathered barn and a windmill, like something out of a Grant Woods painting.

The talk in newspaper articles for months had been of Monaghan selling the Drummond Island resort. Domino's had been divesting of many properties and the Domino's retreat on Drummond was just one of the many things expected to go.

"The thing we tried to do throughout," Conard said, "was not to become a monster. We had gotten to the point on the paper where we could have become a parody of ourselves. It had cost an awful lot of money—we lost business, lost time. I was trying to do two things: run a cabin service and run a newspaper." He laughed, "And of course trying to fish every minute I could."

Conard, who has returned to some of the stained glass work he once did, said he was interested in living more personally and philosophically. "You go through different stages in your life,

I think." He said that lately he had been learning how to medi-
tate. "This was not something I naturally knew how to do, so
I got a book [on it]."

He seems to have become more intellectual again—"I've
pretty much spent my life trying to figure out what we're doing
here," and he said he was exploring mysticism, ordering books
through the Institute of Noetic Science. "It's not that I feel this
realm is an illusion, but there's obviously a lot more to it,"
Conard said, and he found that the new reading he had been
doing, "seems to account for a world apparently in decline."

He and Margeanne said they had joined a movie club where
they could order videos through the mail. There are no large
video stores on Drummond but Conard said he could order
anything and UPS delivers. "We were movie-starved when we
first joined," Margeanne said, because until VCRs, it had been
decades since either of them had seen movies with any regular-
ity.

Bob Conard talked about how the perch would be running
soon. He talked about the river on Drummond, the Potagannissing, where all the fish come in to spawn: walleye, bullheads,
perch, sunfish, northern pike. "We need to protect that river,"
he said.

Margeanne said the bear population had increased on Drummond, bear now were coming into people's backyards.
Margeanne works in the accounting department at the Northwood Restaurant, and she said when she went to work in the
morning, the bears were often there, waiting for food.

I stayed that night at Drummond Island's Stone House, a
former lumber baron's home that is now a bed and breakfast.
After a long, three-hour Finnish sauna next to the bay, I felt
deeply relaxed and fell asleep that night watching the moon rise
over the lake. Early the next morning I saw three bunnies playing in the yard. Moments later I watched as two small deer,
gentle and shy as wood sprites, came to the water's edge, and
then left. From the dock in front of the house I could see big,
striped fish swimming nonchalantly in the clear, deep water.
This island is "a gem," as it says in their Chamber of Commerce

brochures; maybe more of a diamond in the rough, but a lovely place.

As I rode the ferry back to the mainland, I looked at the string of stepping-stone islands in the distance to the east. One little island after another, more than fifty of them, so I'd been told, as if one could swim or boat or go across the ice from one to the other, ad infinitum.

A call to Margeanne at the Northwood on a cold sunny day at the end of April in 1992 revealed that the weather on Drummond Island on April 27 was also cold and sunny, with just a few leeks up in the woods. "Have you heard?" she asked. Then she told me Domino's had been sold to Denny Bailey, one of the many offspring of the Drummond Island Betsy Seaman clan, relatives of the Mosers and the Seamans and the Baileys for over 150 years, and that he and some partners would be running the resort. "It's a monopoly," Margeanne said, "but local." Nobody knew what had happened to Monaghan, except that the downstate newspapers said he had become "more religious," more involved with the church. I noticed a parallel here to Bob Conard's newfound interest in spiritual matters, and it seemed more than a coincidence that both of them have come out of the controversy on that track.

I asked Margeanne if she could go by the Betsy Seaman Park and see what was written on that plaque. It had been raining to beat the cards that day in November when I'd been there and I hadn't taken the time to write it down. Of course, I hadn't thought I'd ever want to know verbatim what it said, but now I guessed I did.

Bob Conard called me later that night, saying he had the words, and also telling me that he was now doing fulltime stained glass work. "I had the best year I've ever had last year," he said. "Margeanne has been totally, 100 percent supportive. I feel very fortunate to be where I am, with who I'm with, doing what I'm doing."

Then he gave me the words on the rock: "Betsy Seaman, 1820–1896, first permanent woman settler on Drummond Island, came here in 1853 with her husband Daniel Murray Seaman who died in 1863—'courageously they wrought, joyously they lived'—She brought up 11 children under difficult pioneer conditions, giving them, without benefit of, without aid of school or church, the cultural teachings that she had enjoyed in her childhood in Canada. Their idealism, helpfulness and hospitality have become the traditions of Drummond Island."

I decided Betsy Seaman may have been the one who triumphed in the end. People die, but ideas and ways of perceiving and doing can stay. It's something no one had considered when Tom Monaghan and Bob Conard had been shadowboxing in the newspapers about what was to become of Drummond Island.

If through Betsy Seaman's legacy every child on Drummond Island will still be fed and educated—and if through Conard's raising the environmental issues the fishery will be protected, and if Monaghan's corporate retreat can become a solid part of the island economy—then the pioneer values of kindness, cooperation, speaking out, and tolerance that defined the integrity and character of democracy in the Drummond Island community will continue into the next century much as they have for the last.

The idea that what one ordinary woman such as Betsy Seaman believes and does can make a difference over one hundred and fifty years later is something one would like to have faith in—as one straps metaphorical calves onto sleds to pay the proverbial dentists of the world in one's own ordinary existence—and so I'd like to think that on Drummond what one is seeing these days, as the result of Betsy Seaman's efforts, is the proof.

Tent Ladies

I have a friend named O. who lived in a tent last summer in order to save on the rent. This is not so unusual, except that she did it with four children and no husband.

O. is beautiful; you should know that much about her. When she wears her sunglasses on top of her head I think she looks a little like Amelia Earhart. She has a nursing degree from one of the best universities in the country. She is petite, and she has a lot of energy.

She has sad eyes and wonderful smile lines. Her father is a doctor; her brothers are lawyers. She grew up well-to-do and Catholic. Her family couldn't accept the idea that she was divorced and destitute and so they dealt with it by not seeing her. She became invisible to them. You might think this sort of thing only happens in old China, not in new America, but I personally know of hundreds of women who have become invisible to their families.

The afternoon I visited the campsite, O.'s friend A., an artist, was there, up from Ann Arbor for the weekend. A., also single, also with two children, also poor, is the daughter of a college professor. A.'s parents offered more moral support when A. became single, but A. was on welfare while she was finishing college because she had no other way to maintain herself and her children.

I am not using their names because it's illegal to live in a tent—against the zoning ordinance—and because they would not want their employers, their families, or their caseworkers to know how they have survived, how they have cut corners.

It is interesting that no one knows how a woman alone with four children makes it and even more interesting that no one asks. The reason, I think, is obvious: no one wants to know. People must assume that Red Riding Hood, no matter how very good she is, as in the song, keeps the wolf from the door in a variety of ways.

O. wears her dark hair in a bun at the nape of her neck. She reminds me of my grandmother, who was born in the Michigan wilderness in 1868. My grandmother also wore her dark hair in a bun at the nape of her neck and was also tiny and determined. She had to be to have nine children, help clear land, build a log home on the Michigan frontier, keep a garden, and have all her children thrive in a day and place when many died.

But O. is on a frontier of a different kind. She is a single mother in a generation when half of us are. O. has a genius for making a home out of next to nothing, raising chickens, networking, bartering, and creative fiscal survival that would make anyone marvel.

Last June, tired of paying over half her monthly income to a landlord, she took her savings and made a down payment on a piece of land. "I can live there for the summer," she said, and she did. She quit her job. "My children need me desperately," she said. "They're all going to turn into drug addicts or criminals if I don't spend some time with them."

Her land was in a round valley. It was rimmed by trees on hills. There were some crooked old apple trees to the south and a slope of second-growth maples on the west.

The day I visited, it was suppertime in July and the sun was casting late shadows. All in the grass around the tents was the sound of crickets, just like the sound track from an old Lassie movie.

O. is a city girl. Maybe not at heart, but by upbringing. I asked her what it was like to sleep outside. "At first," she said, "the night sounds seemed so loud. I would hear crashing in the brush, or hear an animal visit the campsite and it would keep me awake because I'd be afraid. Now all those sounds lull me to sleep."

Around her three tents—a storage tent, a sleeping tent, and a dining tent—there were paths through the grass from the clothesline to the tent, from the portasan to the clothesline, from the campfire to the car. Grass paths, grass doorways.

There was something ancient, timeless, universal, and recognizable about those paths through the grass.

Americans are pioneers once again, after a fashion, but this time not crossing the prairie, and this time with no men around. Just women and children.

Germany after the Second World War was a nation of women alone. I read a novel once where the author describes how eerie it was to visit a German war widow's apartment: there would be the ubiquitous portrait of the young soldier on the top of the bureau or the radio or the whatnot shelf, in the home of an aging woman raising a child or two in dire poverty. And there were hundreds upon hundreds of homes and apartments like this in Germany after the war.

Here in the hills of northern Michigan in the early 1990s, the men are merely absent, not dead. But the talk around the campfire—of domestic treason and desertion under fire—makes one wonder how many women around the country are living in this postwar condition.

Both of these women have boyfriends, and a gallows humor about their plight. "Men are not exactly lining up from here to the road for a couple of poverty-stricken single mothers with oodles of kids," O. said, "not the kind of men you want, anyway."

O. asked A. if they should set the table for supper inside or outside the screen tent.

A. said, "I don't know. It's your house."

I looked around at this house.

Down by the firepit there were plastic folding lawn chairs. Holly Near was on the boombox. A Nancy Drew mystery was lying folded face down on a log. The cat, Kittie Cucumber, roamed the place in that unself-conscious, territorial way cats have. Bikes were lying here and there and everywhere. Swim-

suits and towels hung on the clothesline. Several of the children had gone to cut marshmallow sticks.

O. was wearing a silver hair ornament, and as it caught the light I began to compliment her, saying "You have something in your hair. . . ."

Before I could finish my sentence and say how lovely it looked in the sunlight, O. started patting her head. "Is it *food*?" she asked. Her face looked stricken.

I explained to her that I had just been about to compliment her on her hair ornament. We both laughed and as I walked away I realized that so used was she to cooking, keeping track of small children—and so used was she to having food in her hair; or something equally inappropriate—that she must have experienced the shock of this before: suddenly catching a glimpse of her hair in a mirror and seeing that there were Cherrios in it.

Later around the fire, I composed an impromptu poem: Clown eyes, circus face / Tents setting up on the outskirts of town in the early predawn / All the single moms in the world / Pounding stakes, cleaning the elephants' cages / Falling in love / with sword-swallowers, jugglers, trapeze artists, magicians / In their line of work / What other kind can they meet?

"The good thing about living this way for me," O. said, "is just having things basic and simple. I notice things. The wind. The stars at night. The kids have been enchanted by falling stars. The campfire has drawn people—friends just show up—it's the kind of thing you dream of happening. The campfire seems to relax people, allows them to open up and talk about their real lives.

"The awful things for me have been shopping, sometimes three or four times a day. I would like a place to shower and wash my hair. I can't even begin to keep the kids clean. The smell of the outhouse can get real bad. Rain. When you want to snuggle in and there's no place to snuggle in—not with five kids in a tent."

Five kids?

"Well, I'm counting myself. This is kind of like Swiss Family Robinson. Trying to make something out of not too much.

"But the closeness to nature is incredible. The birds. I don't think I've ever heard so many birds. It's just being submerged in it constantly. I will miss this. When we move inside for the winter, into a house. And I will always remember it. Even when I build my house here, I will sometimes sleep outside and live outside I think, just to know this again."

Later O. took a nursing job and moved into a house in town. She was recognized by her employer as being a person of ability and potential and given special training so that she could administer a new AIDS and sex education program. She said she loved the land in the valley but it was unrealistic to think of living there. A. stayed downstate and although she graduated from college, could not find a teaching job in her field and is working instead in a shelter for the homeless. The land in the valley is up for sale.

I went back to visit the valley one day in October. The September rains had made the grass grow and the grass paths were almost invisible. There was nothing there to indicate O.'s tenancy on the land. Surveyors' stakes marked the boundaries of the property, their neon orange plastic ribbons fluttering in the wind.

Storm Light on
Bois Blanc Island

This is an island that could wash away in a storm is my one thought about Boblo, as a fierce wind tries to blow us from our narrow path and into the raging waters of Lake Huron a few feet away.

Boblo, or Bois Blanc, is a small sandspit of an island off Cheboygan and "us" is me and two people I'd met briefly on the ferry a few hours earlier. And have just run into them again, walking along the shore with their little dog, Spike.

Spike is making good progress. The other three of us are barely holding our own. The wind is incredibly loud. The sound is like that of a train. Invisible. In the air.

Bob McCoy is a stocky, curly haired, well-spoken, young-looking and elegantly dressed man who says he has taken an early retirement from the family business and now spends his time traveling between his Chicago and Boblo homes. Taffy McCoy, his sister, is plainly dressed, a professor of sociology; her area of expertise is the sociology of mental illness, the process of who decides who is insane in this society. Spike, who looks like a poodle mutt, is in fact, Taffy tells me, a rare breed of French canine, a bichon frise.

We are on an ancient, concrete sidewalk that runs between the beach and a row of abandoned-looking, turn-of-the-century summer cottages up the bank. The sidewalk goes for a ways

and then, where it has become crumbled by age or covered by sand, disappears and then picks up again a few feet further on.

I had noticed Bob and Taffy McCoy on the boat because I had been humming—so happy had I been to be on a ferry and facing into open water and unaware that anyone saw or heard me—and had glanced up to find someone looking at me and they had smiled at me, spontaneously, in a rather bemused and kindly way. There had only been a few passengers on the ferry and a bearded captain named Virgil.

On the ferry crossing that morning the air had been gray and humid and the waters of Lake Huron pale and placid with an oily, greenish cast. Now the lake beside us—technically the Straits of Mackinac here—is wildly dark and troubled, roaring with waves, and above us and around us there is an exciting but disquieting mixture of brilliant sunlight and black clouds, both.

Up the bank the row of cottages facing the lake looks disconcertingly unchanged since the early 1900s, almost more like photographs of cottages than actual cottages, and as we walk the time seems to become other, as if I've slipped, or the place has, into another plane of reality or time. Even Bob McCoy, who describes himself as a bon vivant and a raconteur seems to belong to an earlier, more leisurely period in American resort culture.

The wind is so strong it is almost capable of holding us in place. Later I will learn it got up to fifty-five miles per hour that afternoon, but at the time it just seems fantastic, a tropism, an entity unto itself, like nothing I've ever encountered before, and a part of the place.

This is the kind of weather in which ships go down in the Great Lakes, and we are all giddy as one of us reminds the others of the girl whose car blew off the Mackinac Bridge a couple of years earlier, like a scrap of paper, one of the newspapers had reported, and into three hundred feet of dark water below.

Bob and Taffy tell me their father began bringing their family here thirty years ago. "We came here when there was no electricity," Bob says, "no phones." Their brother drowned while sailing off Boblo some years earlier, they tell me, and their memory of that brother and their attachment to the island keeps them coming back.

Bob spends his time reading, walking, cooking, and entertaining the rare houseguest. Taffy comes up when she can, often bringing gourmet food items from downstate and her research materials. "We do a lot of cooking," Bob says. "Supper can take all day."

I ask them how many people like themselves are on Bois Blanc, telling them I have just come from the island's one-room schoolhouse, where Lani White is the teacher for four students, all boys, one of whom calls her "Mom." When a man came to the door with the mail, two boys said, "It's Uncle Al."

Each student had work that was individualized to their particular needs. In the back corner a student at a computer keyboard clicked away behind a partition. Lani White agreed that she has what most would regard as the best of both worlds: modern teaching tools and small class size in a beautiful island setting. She said they could finish the standard curriculum in less time than it would take her in an ordinary classroom, and it gave them time for the exploration of subjects in greater variety and greater depth. She said she had taught downstate for years and missed having other teachers to talk to but treasured the time with the students and the natural resources of the island.

I whiled away the afternoon seated at a tiny desk next to an enormous wasp nest that Lani told me "Uncle Al" had found on the island. At recess the students played with garter snakes, giving the snakes rides down the slide.

Bob gives me a thumbnail sketch of the sociology of the island saying that there are two primary groups, the summer residents who have second homes on the island and the people who live there all year. The population in the summer he estimates to be about two hundred people, and he thinks there are about forty permanent winter residents. He says islanders often marry each other and even when they get divorced, if they remarry, it's often someone from the island. Everyone seems to be related in some way. There are many tourists in the summer who come over on the ferry for the day or for a few days, but in the off-season the island is blessedly peaceful and quiet.

We don't talk then for a while, the wind is so loud. I follow Bob's glance toward a small sandy road and next to it a big field of grass, blowing. The wind riffles the grass and smooths it, like animal fur, making ripples in it. Meanwhile, the clouds above are creating marbleized and shifting shadows on the grass below. It is mesmerizing.

We bore into the wind, using our heads to make a path for our bodies. A sudden shift in the sky, and the sun shatters the cloud cover, throwing light a thousand ways. Distant thunder roars like jets at a county fair. The lake looks like it could eat us alive, if it could only crawl up onto the shore where we are.

There is a wide, soft-looking, cornmeal-colored beach that extends as far as one can see in either direction. Bob and Taffy say there is good swimming "in the summer." August is barely over as we speak, and so I divine that summer is the key word here.

What is it like here in the winter?

"Winter is a challenge," Bob says. "What they do is take a line of trees [and place them in holes in the ice between Bois Blanc and Cheboygan]. If the trees stand up, you can go across. If the trees are laying down, you can't go across. Last year two people drowned. They were crossing at night and they got off the tree line and they splashed into the Straits." Their bodies came up in the spring.

This has been my year for islands and the people who live on them. I can't get enough of them. I think I am looking for the islands in my own psyche, the lost and undiscovered parts of myself.

I have fantasized about islands—not so much as places to live or places to escape to—but the comings and goings, the ferry rides, attract me. I see in my mind the way the boat leaves the harbor, then I see the open water, then finally we lose sight of the land behind us and there is nothing but sky and water before us, then slowly the island reveals itself on the horizon and we come bumping at last into the dock; then I want to go and take that ride on that boat to that island, and then I do.

Islands are places where you can be changed—like Circe's island where Odysseus' men were changed into animals—and then changed back again. Where you can transform yourself into someone else, or imagine you can.

Islands are not the mainland, so by definition they are not bound to the same rules as the mainland. One of Shakespeare's last plays, *The Tempest,* where all manner of magical things happen, is set on an island. Thomas More's *Utopia,* about a perfect community, is set on an island and became such a classic it added the word and the concept to our language. Thomas Mann's metaphysical *Death in Venice* begins on an island and continues, through several boat rides and gondola journeys, in a watery Venice of the soul. Aldous Huxley's fictional Will Farnaby, dying of the disease called Civilization, goes to rejuvenate himself on an island in the book called *Island,* and the real-life painter Paul Gauguin spent much of the last third of his life living and painting on South Sea Islands. There must be something to it, this craving for islands.

I think it's in part that our civilization is moving so quickly into new realms, where picture phones, human clones, virtual reality games, and travel by trains running on magnetic tape tracks in the air are just around the corner, and where we daily contend with things unimaginable twenty years ago or even twenty weeks ago—ceaseless voice mail, e-mail, car phones, modems, computerized shopping, handitellers—that our so-called modern conveniences, our sorcerers' apprentices, have sometimes seemed to all conspire to create a pace like centrifugal force that spins us until we see ourselves flying out or up or back into the quietness of an island where the world of before seems to still exist and we can reestablish that ancient connection between ourselves and the universe.

"There's a log home Yves St. Laurent would *kill* for," Bob says in diva tones, indicating an elaborately built log cottage— the kind the Rockefellers built in the Rockies a century ago— "but I could put my walking stick through any *part* of it: it's so porous [from insects]."

Bob says a small colony of artists, including a few musicians from the Chicago Symphony, were here at one time but, with the exception of one or two, they died or moved away years ago and have not been replaced by other summer residents. Waste disposal on the island is a problem; the island dump has been closed. The cost of getting things to the island and off the island is high. "There are no new people moving in. Houses don't go on the market. The property stays in the family. I bought my house from my father." He estimates that 80 percent of the island is in the hands of the state (54 percent of the island is state-owned, the other 46 percent is privately owned but about half of this acreage is heavily restricted by state and federal environmental laws, I learned later) and that the other 20 percent "is in the hands of a very few people who are not motivated to sell."

Bois Blanc Island is only twelve miles long and seven miles wide and today it *feels* small. I can feel the edges of it, sense its size in the intensity of wind and the sound of the water, can imagine myself walking its circumference, can imagine knowing all the people here by name within a week.

We move from the walk along the waterfront to a path through tall pines. There is a thick carpet of pine needles beneath my feet. It is dark under the evergreens and quieter here farther from the shore. It begins to rain lightly. Taffy says she fantasizes about this island as their secret hideaway, a place to come if the bomb drops.

We pass an Episcopal church where the gray cobblestones of a homemade archway fatten in the rain. Then we continue on down past several boarded-up cottages closed for the season and then onto a mossy, gravelly trail to the McCoys's.

Bob McCoy has redone "the children's cottage" in his family, and the narrow walk to it is bordered with tiny, brightly colored flowers. As we go up the steps to the screened porch, a young male houseguest skips sideways satyrlike down the front steps, followed by clouds of steam scented with bay leaf, off to the store before it closes to get some cooking ingredient.

Inside it is all deep blue-greens, light pine floors, reading nooks with soft cushions in designer fabrics in muted shades of blue-green. "It never looked like this when we were growing up here," Bob says when I compliment him on his decorating. "This was where we put all the cousins when they came."

I passed one small store on Boblo open at this time of year, and it sells everything from bait to diapers; no fresh fruit or vegetables were in evidence. I'd been told the post office is the center of social life, and the bar. Other than some commercial fishing and some harvesting of maple syrup, there's no commerce to speak of; there's no industry, no hospitals, no judges, no lawyers, no courts, no libraries, no art galleries, no laundromat. It is a sweetly undeveloped and softly beautiful place.

"It's easy to lose track of time here," Bob jokes. "Line up ten people and ask everyone what day it is—if two people agree, then that's what day it is."

He offers me a cup of coffee. "Boblo" is how islanders pronounce Bois Blanc, he says. On the mainland, before I arrived, I heard it pronounced "Bwha Blanch" and "Boys Blank" and everything in between. It is a French phrase and I was told on Bois Blanc that it meant "white wood" for the birch trees everywhere. I later heard that Bois Blanc was a French Canadian term for the American basswood and that that might be the now-forgotten origin of the name.

Bob hands me an old sepia-toned brochure that shows two handsome men in knickers in a wooded setting. He says it is a remnant from the island's former Wilderness Club, a rustic but high-toned, turn-of-the-century club for the very wealthy. People came up the big lakes by steamer to stay there for a week or for the entire summer.

He gives me a Wilderness Club menu for Sunday dinner, which, along with prime rib and roast lamb, includes such delicacies as boiled ox tongue and green apple pie. The one puzzling item on the menu is "reception flakes," which we speculate might be some early version of Wheaties.

The Wilderness Club brochure is written in a breezy manner, with dozens and dozens of connecting clauses, reminiscent of what Gertrude Stein called her "money" style, in which she wrote for magazines when she toured America in the 1930s.

"The Wilderness Club is composed of men who invite kindred spirits who want to live more fully; men, who through the exactions of the hours of business subconsciously perhaps, anticipate the day . . . when they may throw their cares away and live close to Nature—out in 'the open,' men who have not as yet become so deeply entrenched in today's forced and unnatural manner of living and striving to accomplish, that they have entirely lost interest in the broad uncultivated fields. . . men who want to be boys again, to 'let down,' to give vent to the spirit of play . . . to romp, to swim, to fish, to stroll about in Nature's playground unhampered and unsought."

Aside from the question as to what reception flakes might be, what happened to the people who ate them? Where did the men in knickers, men who want to be boys, go?

Bob tells me the Wilderness Club burned down. He asks if I recall seeing a large, grassy area near the road and when I nod, he says, "That's where it was."

When Michigan was first opened for settlement in the 1830s, many homesteaders lived on islands. Islands were more accessible and inhabitable than anywhere else and provided an instant livelihood in fishing and a steady income in cutting cordwood for the steamers that plied the lakes. After that the ships went to coal and oil fuel instead of wood, and simultaneously, the interior of Michigan developed more roads and became more settled. By the 1890s the population on the majority of the various Michigan islands was dwindling and by the 1950s, many of the islands had been all but abandoned. The 1990s has seen a resurgence of interest in islands, largely because by the 1980s lake frontage on the mainland had become both prohibitively expensive and extremely hard to acquire.

After a short time, I thank the McCoys for the coffee and for showing me the Wilderness Club brochure and go back out into the strange rain-and-sunshine afternoon. Travel makes me feel stimulated and enervated at the same time, exhausted by learning new things and excited by it. Now I am feeling a strong need to find my motel room and be alone for a while. I make my way back down the small sandy road that leads to the one-room schoolhouse so that I can retrieve my satchel of books and my duffel bag.

The sandy road to the school has a ribbon of lavender-tinged light above it. Only five months before I had been home on the Leelanau walking behind my house on an old logging trail in which there had been hundreds of small milky-purple butterflies floating in the path like a low, living cloud. With a jolt I realize I've thought of this because the path of sky above me is the exact pale, blue-violet shade of those lepidoptera.

Behind me, at the shore end of the road, the lake roars. The sound surges down the road in waves that wash and eddy around me like water.

The school's shed entranceway smells of the rubber of indoor-outdoor carpet and the mildew of old wooden walls, bringing back memories of the smell of wet galoshes in the cloakroom of my own days at the small old red brick schoolhouse in Glen Arbor. "Kid Zone," reads a poster with a smiling turtle, his amphibious hand raised in greeting. Under it are the words, "Enter with Care and Love."

I stand in the warm, stale air of the shed, out of the wind, while the dusk deepens in the pine woods around the school. I stare momentarily at a child's worn, red jacket hanging on a hook. There is a poem above it, written in flowing script. "If once you have slept on an island," this poem by Rachel Field begins, "You'll never be quite the same. / Oh, you won't know why, and you can't say how / Such change upon you came, / But once you have slept on an island, / You'll never be quite the same."

For a moment I feel the child's jacket could be mine, or my child's, the time of the poem—from the early 1900s—the time I live in. Lately I've begun to suffer from a terrifying sense that I am a ghost in my own life, a doppelgänger of myself or past life versions of myself or some other person, and I can't tell if this is because I'm in transition, or is an aspect of travel itself, or because past lives have become a metaphor for the pace of modern life.

A *New Yorker* cartoon recently showed two earnest daters, and one says to the other, "I wasn't anybody in a previous lifetime either." We can only imagine that this was offered, and received, as reassurance.

Outside the schoolyard is quiet in the gathering shadows of late afternoon. The bare sandy loam smells sour, the way schoolyard sand smells when it's been played in forever. Here, only a few hours earlier, garter snakes took rides down the slide. I glance back at the school. Lani White said the snakes live in the foundation. There is still a strong wind. I can hear it like loud bees in the trees above my head and there is that terrifying dull roar of the waters of Lake Huron washing up the tree-tunnel road, like the sound in a culvert.

As I drive, the pines along the narrow two-track from the school slowly sway like grass or ferns—like the giant prehistoric gymnosperms that they in fact are—first far in one direction, and then far in the other.

This is a seriously potholed road and I make my way along it cautiously, not daring to drive more than ten miles an hour. Where, I wonder, do they fix cars on this island? The air, washed by the storm, is pale and bright. There are stands of birches here, mournful and white as ghosts, their wispy branches sweeping the ground like old women's hair.

Perhaps a mile beyond the ferryboat dock, a large tree falls across the road. It is just inches in front of my car. It shakes the ground. It shakes me. After a minute or two, I get out and look at it, feeling even as I do absurdly helpless: there's no way I can move this tree. My father always traveled with an ax in his car—and knew how to use it. I should have learned when he wanted to teach me. I manage to get around the tree by going through the woods, nearly tearing the oil pan off the bottom of my car as I do.

My motel, adjoined by a restaurant and party store, is on the water in a dark stand of trees. The store is closed. The restaurant is open, but empty. The glassed-in kitchen is dark. I see only my shadow, darkly reflected. There is a black pay phone on the wall and on a chalkboard there's a sign that announces that dinner tonight will be spaghetti. I stand waiting, wondering what to do.

The soul, I think, staring past and through my own reflection and into the darkened kitchen, must be micalike, must look like a mirror, if it looks like anything, and fill with light and become drained of light, as the person does.

I move toward the tables and chairs in the center of the room. Then I get my briefcase of books from the car. These are books I've brought with me and some new ones I've just bought at Cheboygan's Logmark Bookstore. The Logmark Bookstore was astonishingly sophisticated, more like the Gotham Bookstore in Manhattan, even to the distracted and bespectacled booksellers, than anything one would expect to find in a faded lakeshore town three hundred miles north of Detroit.

I get myself a cup of tepid coffee from the pot that's sitting at the side of the room. I feel terrifyingly tiny, so small a bird could swallow me. I feel myself waver and place my hand, palm down, on the cool formica top of the sideboard for a moment before making my way to a table.

I sit in one of the plastic chairs at the table and look out onto the water, where the storm is raging. I read Blake. I read Homer. What does it matter that I nearly died from a tree landing on me? Across thousands of years I transcend the illusory closed horizons of place and time by associating with other minds.

Since this is also where I am to get my key to my room for the night, I just keep waiting, and reading, thinking surely someone will come. Finally, after a half hour or so, I decide to call the number in the phone book that I had called to get the reservation in the first place, a week earlier.

I am relieved when someone answers and says they'll be right down. While I am talking on the phone to them I am reading a sign on the board next to the phone that says: "WANTED—woman to Cook and Clean fish, dig Worms and make lures. Must have GOOD BOAT and motor. Please enclose picture of boat and motor." I had seen this first several weeks earlier in the Northland Restaurant on Drummond and more recently at the Engadiner in Engadine on Route 2 in the Upper Peninsula; it had been mildly amusing then, but by now time and repetition have flattened its humor to a point of diminishing returns.

I wait quite a while. I had told them on the phone, when they asked, that I would probably want supper—thinking that maybe ten people would show up or at least the members of their family, but no one comes.

I am shaking and feel very cold. It occurs to me that I might be in shock. The tree missed me by moments. No one is coming and it's getting dark.

Finally the woman arrives and gives me the key to my room. I pay for the room and the coffee, and tell her I am going on down the shore to the only other public place on the island, the Bois Blanc Tavern, which I've heard is a few miles further on.

"Can't miss it!" she says. She seems relieved not to have to make me supper. "Right on the road!"

The road is alternately dark with puddles and in other places gleaming white with puddle-sized lozenges of newly washed gravel, all from the hard rain; *the road looks like a Dalmatian,* I think. Here the shore of the island is much rockier. In places the gravel road is very close to the gravel shore, and almost indistinguishable from it.

The Bois Blanc Tavern is a long, low, weather-stained slabwood structure. Across the road is a gravelly and marshy escarpment into Lake Huron, startlingly pristine and wild, in contrast to the bar. Now, again, the sun is out, but the storm-wracked waters of the lake do not create a mellow mood. The bar parking lot has room for thirty vehicles, but today there are only three, all of them trucks.

A strong wind blows a very large, hospital-refuse-blue, empty plastic barrel all the way across the wide sweep of gravel parking lot during the entire time I am walking from my car to the wooden ramp up to the front door. The barrel on the gravel makes a light musical sound, reminiscent of the Caribbean, the Rastifarians, an oddly tropical touch here on the shores of northern Lake Huron during a storm.

Inside a very nice lady who looks like Dolly Parton welcomes me to sit next to her at the bar. She is as willing to talk as I am needing to talk and she fills me in on the island lore as I sip a Diet Coke. There are about ten people here, mostly men who mostly look like country and western singers. They have no coffee here and people on both sides of the bar seem surprised that I don't order an alcoholic drink.

I know little or nothing about bar etiquette and wonder if I *should* order a drink. I couldn't feel much more out of my element if I had stepped into the intergalactic bar in *Star Wars.* I am considering ordering a drink to relax me, when my mind flashes back to that time a few months earlier when I was a guest speaker at a ladies book club in a southern Michigan city, and two glasses of white wine and club soda worked like truth serum.

All the book club ladies wanted to share—as ladies love to do, so a midwife friend of mine tells me—and since I was the guest, they just kept asking me question after question. Each of my answers triggered another raging round of questions—they'd never heard of anything like that in their lives or met anybody like me, ever. When they were done I was a damp spot on the carpet and the book tour was over.

"Thanks," I say. "I think I'll hold off on the drink."

Then the barmaid, Susie White, the sister of Lani White's husband, offers me an "initiation drink." She says it will be on the house, a Boblo tradition for first-time visitors.

I tell her I'll take a rain check, and she gives me a second Diet Coke on the house instead. It's the off season and the bar doesn't serve food but Susie offers to make something. The only thing available here before "boat day" later in the week is a frozen hamburger, which I gratefully order without the bun, and a side of dill pickles.

No one asks me where I'm from or what I'm doing on the island. I think this is politeness, but it turns out that they have all known all about me since I got off the ferry. They believe I am there to write about their island; I believe it myself at that point.

I love the feeling of camaraderie, the ordinary conversation that goes on around me, the talk of gardens that got frosted and trees that came down in the wind and a deer that got lost on the ice the winter before.

They tell me I should see Victor Babcock, the man whose great-grandparents settled the island. They look for the phone book so I can call him, but then, not finding it, it turns out everyone there knows Victor Babcock's phone number by heart anyway. Someone dials for me and before I know it I have plans to see the Babcocks at eight o'clock that night.

There were forty people on the island the winter before, they tell me. Then they dispute that. Maybe it was thirty-seven. Maybe it was forty-two. Someone has found the phone book while this conversation is going on: there is a scant one and one-third pages devoted to Bois Blanc Island.

They go through the list, naming people who left for a while and came back, taking the count all over again. They are like expatriots in Paris in the 1920s, except that they are here on a Michigan island in the early autumn of 1991. They are fixed income retirees, laid-off auto workers, woodcutters, artists, young people with no attachments, modern-day expatriots, the kind one finds in every outpost of America and maybe the globe, waiting out the storm in more ways than one.

Some now work, on and off the island, in construction. One man says he has a friend on the island who just got back from working a big construction job in Saipan. Susie White and some of the younger people with no savings, pension, or other income will go downstate for the winter and work.

No one here has children in the school, although clearly there are at least four children on the island. These people have raised their children, if they had any. They talk about how hard it was to raise children in cities. They talk about the crime and violence, the woman they knew who's child was kidnapped from her front yard, the man who was mugged in the parking lot of Farmer Jack's and was never able to walk again. Many were working two and three jobs when they lived in the Detroit area, commuting long distances; they say they hardly ever saw their spouses or children because working and commuting took up all of their time. Many are now divorced. A few remarried shortly before or after coming to the island.

In the winter, they tell me, there are potlucks at the tavern fairly often. They put a big piece of plywood over the shuffleboard game and thus convert it to a long table and everyone brings a dish to pass. In January the bar closes and people get together for breakfast potlucks at each other's houses Sunday mornings.

"There's compassion for your neighbor," Scott Galbraith says.

"We fight and feud," Greg Smith says, "but if you broke your leg, your worst enemy would be over there the next morning cuttin' your wood for the winter."

"You got to," someone down the bar says. "You couldn't live with yourself if you didn't."

An older blond lady with a deep, Mae West voice says, "There'll come a time when you might need someone to help you, so that's in your mind when you go to help someone else."

Someone looks out at the stormy waters and says something about "the witch of November," making reference to the Gordon Lightfoot song about the sinking of the Edmund Fitzgerald with all the men on board on Lake Superior and the line, "when the witch of November comes early."

Someone says the ferry has stopped running and might not run in the morning. Someone says there's a tree down in the road.

Sheriff Edgar Arnett comes in, the island's sole law enforcement officer, and someone asks him about the tree. He says he cut it up and moved it. Someone else says they heard on their scanner the wind is blowing fifty-two miles per hour. Someone else says they rode that afternoon in a private boat across from Cheboygan in six-foot seas. The speaker is a large, burly man. Someone asks him how it was and he says, "It was different."

The ferryboat owner comes in, looks at me, and laughs and says, "You plan on leavin' in the mornin'?"

Clyde Bishop comes in and looks at me and says, "What's *she* doin' here?"

Someone tells him I'm there to see how many people on the island are in the witness protection program.

Clyde tells me there are bald eagles on the island, as well as bobcat, deer, otter, and fox. Apparently there are no skunks, porcupine, or bear on the island, but no one seems to know why; perhaps these animals, which could theoretically cross on the ice as well as any others, are hibernating at that time.

Clyde says there are Michigan rattlesnakes on the island, as well as the garter snakes I saw at the school earlier in the day. "Oh, them rattlers are good eatin'," someone from the end of the bar says. I turn to Janie and Scott Galbraith, who are sitting next to me, "Do people eat the snakes?"

"Yeah, some of 'em do," Scott says. "I've never participated in them myself."

I leave the Bois Blanc Tavern and go back to my motel to

take a shower and rest and read. I turn the heat up as high as it will go. I am still freezing. I get into the motel bed with its polyester coverlet and then I get up again and put on half the clothes I have brought with me. I can't seem to get warm. I get out my books.

On the ferry I had started reading *Gilgamesh* and now get it out again. Gilgamesh is grieving for his friend Enkidu, whom he enticed into battle and who got killed. "No one grieves this much," the barmaid Siduri, who lives in a cottage at the edge of the sea, tells Gilgamesh. "Forget your friend. He is dead."

I find I am crying. I am wet with salty tears. Big waves of grief sweep through me like the contractions of child labor. I am grieving, like Gilgamesh, but I don't know for what. Gilgamesh is sleeping in the river god's house, on the floor while the river god and his shuffling old wife go about their daily affairs. I fall asleep finally, too, a deep, but troubled sleep.

When I awake I am sweating profusely and have kicked all the covers off. I am having trouble breathing. I don't recognize where I am and don't know if I am alive or dead, male or female. I feel someone is sitting on me and only slowly do I realize I have been having a dream of the river god's wife on my chest, her long, gray hair sweeping to and fro over me.

As if rising from beneath an undertow, I stand to turn the heat down. Out behind the motel, there is a dark green rectangle of lawn in front of a rectangular dwelling. I lay back down for a while in gray, post nightmare.

I get up and get dressed. I want to call home. I walk across the road to the restaurant but the pay phone seems to be out of order. I feel more disappointed than the broken phone warrants and force myself to recognize that every day some waitress, some traveling salesman, and four hundred others suffer the same or similar problem. Back outside I am fascinated by the way the storm light seems to create strangely falsified contours in the woods. Even my car looks eerily outlined, as if it has a fine fluorescent border around it.

Night is coming. The storm seems to have subsided. I walk back to my room up the gravel trail and then put my raincoat and notebook in the car to go back to the Babcocks on the other side of the island.

The moon is rising as I drive down the shore road toward the Babcocks. Mine is the only car on the road. The island seems to be in for the night.

I follow the directions Mr. Babcock gave me when I'd talked to him over the phone from the tavern. In behind the one-room school, down the two-track, to the brown house. His wife, 'Berta, invites me in through the back, apologizing for not having me in through the front door, but explaining that the back way is drier.

We go through the kitchen. A black frying pan with a picture of their house hangs on the wall. An artist somewhere did it for them, she says. She takes me in to where her husband, Victor Babcock, a man in his late fifties, is sitting in the living room, a room with overstuffed chairs and afghans.

Victor has never lived anywhere except on Bois Blanc, he says. 'Berta tells me she has been here since she married Victor thirty-five years ago. He has just retired from the Mackinac County road crew, where he was the county's sole island employee. The couple has two grown sons who do not live on the island. These sons went to the one-room school on the island through eighth grade at which time they then went to school in Cheboygan, boarding with friends or relatives through the school year and coming home only for holidays.

"It's awful hard on the kids to go," Victor says of that period of time when his sons left the island for school on the mainland, "awful hard on the folks here, too, having them away. So many things can happen to a child. You want to be there with them."

The older son graduated from Michigan State University and the younger son from Northwestern Michigan College. The older son is in the field of social work, and the younger one reads blueprints for a company that does steel construction work for shopping centers. Neither live on the island, nor could they and have the careers they have or earn the living they do.

The Babcocks found a way to live comfortably on Bois Blanc, but they couldn't find ways for their children to do the same. A simple life, a safe existence, are not so easy to achieve beyond a generation or two, even in a place as uncomplicated as Boblo.

I ask them about the tree line and the snowmobile accident. They tell me what the people at the tavern had told me. That there had been some heavy drinking and the man driving the snowmobile, who was not from the island, did not realize the danger of not sticking to the tree line.

Later Roberta Babcock will write to me and describe in detail the annual ritual of putting up the tree line. "When the island men decide to check the ice for thickness," she writes, "some of them walk across it. They keep checking the thickness of the ice. Some come behind on snowmobiles, if the ice is thick enough—usually six inches thick. Then they cut small pine trees to plant in holes they drill in the ice. One man has a gas line power machine with a large drill bit that drills the holes in the ice. The men bring small trees on trailers behind their snowmobiles, or Hondas, to put in the holes. The trees are put in the ice for safe crossing as you could get lost on the ice in a snow storm or in the fog. The ice can get up to twelve inches or more in thickness."

"My dad made his money moonshinin' and cuttin' wood for Mackinac Island," Victor says that evening. "They had hollow-bottom boats. I guess they'd put the moonshine in the bottom and the wood on top." He said islanders also made their living providing services to the resorters, doing plumbing, carpentry. "You name it. We did it," he says. "Still do."

He tells me about going to another one room school on the island and how the school teacher would cook their lunch on the wood stove while the children were studying their lessons. They sometimes had potato soup and corn meal mush for lunch. "The children would bring raw cut up potatoes and onions, and canned milk for the potato soup," his wife says.

Victor says he wouldn't know how to live anywhere but Boblo. "This way if I want to walk out in the woods, I just walk out my front door." They have a one-hundred-year-old lighthouse on the island, and until 1947 there was a man who lived there and tended it. There are many spots, deep in the island, that only islanders know about, Babcock says, one where there is virgin hemlock and another where there is a virgin stand of pine.

"There's another spot on the island," he says. "We think it happened thousands of years ago—it's just *perfectly round*—where maybe a meteorite hit. Now that's a thing a person oughta see if they had a chance to."

The Babcocks entertain me well into the evening with Bois Blanc Island lore, inviting me back in the spring to see where the meteorite hit. They are like people I knew when I was growing up on the Leelanau Peninsula in the 1950s.

As I drive down the white gravel road, I shut my lights off and just drive. It is almost midnight in pale moonlight: night's noon. I think back to the way the Babcocks walked me out to the car, the way they shook my hand two or three times before I left.

What is it about the Babcocks, I ask myself, that makes them resemble the people I grew up with? They are trusting, I decide. We've lost that, in a world of strangers. People come to Bois Blanc to find that ability to trust again that they once knew in themselves and their fellow humans.

I drive down this empty gravel road on a small island in northern Michigan where all forty of the residents have gone to bed for the night, thinking that we have all been pushing too hard, ourselves, our world.

Pilots call it "pushing the envelope," a way of taking the corner too fast. We all need to find those islands in ourselves, those islands in our world, where things are basically simple and we know our neighbors, and have compassion for them.

The next morning, I am back on the ferry. All my fears from the night before seem as remote as if they'd never existed. The sky is the white, misty sky of early morning, promising a mild day; no dragons plow the mist. It is cold this morning and so I move inside the cabin with the other passengers. They are talking about someone they know who has moved away.

"He's downstate now. Fell *in love* with a woman named Flavia."

"Flavia?"

"Yeah, Flavia, can you imagine bein' in bed and callin' out her name in the night, 'Oh, Flav. Oh, Flavia.'"

The talk turns to the storm the night before.

"I was out here once in ten-foot seas, with water comin' in over the deck and freezin' and the cars rollin'. I'll tell ya, I didn't know whether it was worse to be on the boat or in the water."

"It got pretty roiled up last night."

"The radio said fifty-five miles an hour."

"Who won at cards last night? It was card night for Lani White and them."

Susie White, the bartender from the tavern the night before, says she's going to Cheboygan for the day to see the dentist.

There's an old man in a life vest sitting kitty-corner from her.

"I see you got your life vest on," she says.

"Yep. I never took no chances with no boats."

The old woman next to him says, "He's wore that life vest ever since the dinghy sank."

The old man says, "It was September, late, like about it is now. The water was warmer than the air. We went down; just like that. Sank our groceries, everything. I stayed in that water two hours 'fore they come to fetch me out." He smiles, shakes his head. "But I was a lot younger then."

Susie White laughs. The whole cabin laughs with her.

"I figure if I go down now," the old man taps his life-vest-covered chest, "I'll pop right back up again."

When the ferry docks in Cheboygan, I get in my car and drive it off. It seems suddenly calmer and quieter, as if the wind had been blowing, and now it isn't. Even the ground underfoot seems more solid.

I feel a slight pang of separation. I understand what Susie White was saying moments before, about not wanting to leave for the winter, not wanting to leave even for a day. Their total lives are encapsulated there, like "Days of Our Lives" for real, and there's no newspaper that will give a running account of the days they miss so they can catch up. So that's why they stay. They have made lives for themselves—the McCoys and the Babcocks and the people at the tavern—in which they are real because their neighbors know them. They do not need to be images of themselves for each other. They are who they are without ever saying who they are, and it is this that makes me want to go back to their island and live there, too, that makes me feel as I drive away that the island ceases to exist a little with each mile and each hour. I think it is this quality of illusoriness, of immateriality, of elusiveness that is the essence of what both draws me to islands and sends me away from them, simultaneously and endlessly.

MIGRATIONS

Sugar Island

This could be Louisiana bayou country, so low is this land along the St. Marys River. The island out in the river is just a stone's throw from the shore. In warm weather, if there are no currents here, a person could swim to it.

I glance over at my daughter. We are happy, Gaia and I and our dogs, Crusher and Ginger, to be on a trip like this in bright sunlight, waiting in line at the ferry to go see an unknown island.

"I think we should call our mouse Reepicheep," Gaia says when I pull into line behind a red Ford pickup and shut the motor off on our Horizon. She is teasing me.

She looks over from the book she has been reading, *Voyage of the Dawn Treader*, to catch my reaction.

"*Our* mouse?" We had discovered a mouse nest and a stash of peanuts in the glove compartment before we set out on this trip.

"Listen to this," she says now, reading. "This is the Captain of the ship talking, 'But what manner of use would it be ploughing through all this blackness?' And Reepicheep says, 'Use, Captain? . . . So far as I know we did not set sail to look for things useful but to seek honour and adventures.'"

It had been my idea to entice the mouse out tonight—aren't mice nocturnal?—by moving the peanuts outside the car while we slept. "Put the book away for awhile. Let's see where we are."

To the side of us is a field with a chain link fence around it.

Inside the fence is a crumbling old sidewalk that leads up to an ancient lighthouse. Beyond that, the quietness of the river.

As we wait for the ferry we glance at the people in the other cars. "That girl looks a little like me," Gaia observes absently, "in the red car." I look and there is a teenager who looks a little like Gaia.

"She does," I say, looking in my rearview mirror. "What about the man in the black pickup truck? Does he look like your father? Don't stare," I add, as I realize the man saw me look at him. "You can see him in your side view mirror."

"Yeah," she says after looking without appearing to, "he looks like Dad." I cringe inwardly for a moment, thinking about how I am trying to spot Native Americans the way someone might try to find hummingbirds, or rare orchids, but then I think that that's not too far off the mark, and nothing that diminishes their inherent worth or humanity is meant by it. Gaia is, after all, half Ottawa. Her father and I are divorced, but have a genial and polite relationship. He does take her to powwows, but this trip is not a powwow. I want her to see people who look like her just living their lives. I hadn't told her, because I didn't want her to be disappointed if it didn't happen, but I'm hoping to find that on Sugar Island.

I begin laughing at the absurdity of it all, and Gaia begins laughing, too. She understands immediately. "Oh, look," she says, "I think I spy one." We laugh together for a minute, then lapse into silence.

I had first heard about Sugar Island from Edgar Arnett, the sheriff on Bois Blanc Island off Cheboygan where I had visited a few weeks earlier. Arnett had said the Sugar Island population was mostly Indians. Without telling Gaia why exactly I wanted to go to Sugar Island, I had said maybe we'd go there sometime.

It is one of those trips you take because the weather is supposed to be good that weekend and because you have a pull to go. With the five-hundred-year-anniversary of Columbus's arrival in the New World just around the corner, Gaia's fifth grade class has had more classroom activities than usual centered around Columbus. "He opened up trade with the New World," she had said her teacher told them, imitating her teacher's voice, a voice perpetually filled with boundless enthusiasm, and Gaia said she had wanted to say, "But what about us?" And did she, I had asked. "No," she said, "she wouldn't have gotten it."

From her social studies book she had quoted for me how Columbus was greeted in the New World by "friendly" Indians—"whom he tortured," she ad-libs. She wanted to show me the passage and I looked. I saw also that she had defaced the picture of Columbus, making a strange trapezoid over his mouth. I didn't say anything. I didn't know what to say. I don't want her to love Columbus. I don't want her to hate her teacher. I don't want her to feel voiceless.

It takes only a few moments to cross this part of the St. Marys River once our car is on the ferry. We follow the other cars off and up a high hill straight in front of us. The clouds are wispy and Gaia says they resemble the thin strands of cotton candy when the lady is making it in the booth at the fair.

At the top of the hill we can see that this island is *big*. Gaia finds in a brochure where it says Sugar Island is sixteen miles long and nine miles wide in the middle, about forty-five square miles altogether. The woods and fields here are cultivated and old, like New England. We are the only car on the road for long, long periods of time. Those who pass us seem to live here.

We see a narrow, tall, old brick house on the water, like an inn from two hundred years ago. In front of it on a wide, sandy lawn above the water are six husky dogs, each with its own doghouse, now all barking at us and our dogs. The car is a cacophony of resounding barks, answered by the barks outside.

There appears to be no one here. I pull out again and further on down the road stop and ask directions of men in duck hunter's camouflage. We have a reservation for the night at a resort, and I show him where it is on my map. We are told to go back the way we came, down the gravel road, past the woods, and past the place where the road seems to become a two-track.

We do, and find a series of rustic, 1950s-style cabins set back under tall, skinny trees. The trees are dark vertical lines, like bars of a giant cage, through which there are a series of long, narrow, parallel, light blue, vertical views of the water. I am dizzy looking at this. Finally I pick out a trailer that says, "Office." A woman comes to the door. She introduces herself as Grace and walks us over to our cabin.

The cabin is so much like one our family stayed in near Allentown, Pennsylvania, on a trip to Washington, D.C., in 1952 that it's uncanny. When Grace leaves, Gaia and I bring in our sleeping bags and bring in the dogs and light the gas heater to take the chill out of the cabin.

Now we go back to use Grace's phone. I ask her where there is a restaurant where we can have supper and she says at this time of year there are no restaurants open on the island. She sells us some of her own grapefruit juice and a loaf of frozen Italian bread she has made herself.

Grace is attractive, in the carefully coifed, blond manner popular in the early 1960s. She is divorced, she confides. She and her husband moved up from the Detroit area and then he took off with another woman and left her and the children. "At first I thought, 'How will I make it?'" she says. "But I'm better off."

Single moms are everywhere. I am one myself and so often do I run into women alone with children that the country is beginning to seem like an ersatz matriarchy. I can help my daughter avoid polarizing people on the basis of race, or at least I think I can, but how can I help her deal with the more subtle, more pervasive polarity between women and men?

"I just never stopped eating after he left," Grace says, recognizing perhaps that I am single like she is, or perhaps just telling me her story because she needs to tell it. "I got so fat. I stopped cleaning the house. Finally one day my youngest said to me, 'Mom, when are you going to get out of your nightgown?' I hadn't realized. I thought, 'What am I doing to this child?' And so I pulled myself out of it. I was just not thinking of anyone but myself."

I ask her what there is to see on Sugar Island. She tells me to see Duck Island, the estate of a former governor of Michigan,

Chase Osborn. "I haven't seen him," she says. "My son saw him." It takes me a minute to realize she is not talking about Osborn. "He said, 'Dad, why'dya do it?' My husband said, 'Your mom's a good woman, son. Don't you ever forget it.'"

She tells me to call the caretakers at the Osborn estate, Pauline and Ed Andrews, a brother and sister. "They talk loud on the phone," she says, as she dials the number for me and hands me the phone. "It's just the way they talk." Grace tells us about the nondenominational church all the islanders built together, and which we could walk to in the morning from her resort.

Back in our cabin, Gaia and I heat up canned Campbell's soup and drink the grapefruit juice Grace sold us.

We get out the dog food. "Ginger won't eat until Crusher has eaten," Gaia observes.

"Why do you think that is?"

"I think Ginger thinks she's the mom," Gaia says.

"Maybe in dog world, she is," I answer. We have already discussed how there is "people world" and "dog world," with a seemingly different set of givens for each perspective.

I take a shower in the stand-up, tin shower in the bathroom. The water comes out in a trickle but it's good to wash the road dust off and slip into baggy corduroys and an old sweater.

We take Crusher on a leash down along the water and Ginger follows. Ginger doesn't need a leash. She is an old collie, Gaia's first dog, and has long ago taken on the responsibility of watching out for us. *It's a big job, but somebody's gotta do it,* she seems to be always thinking to herself. Crusher, named by the people we got her from for Dr. Beverly Crusher on *Star Trek,* is a young German shepherd who is loyal, smart, eager for training, and lives for physical exercise.

"Ginger controls Crusher with looks," Gaia says. "And she paws Crusher over on her back and kind of nuzzles her stomach, like a mom. If she doesn't want Crusher to go to something, she just blocks the way. Ginger doesn't boss Crusher around, she just makes her want to do the right thing by giving her loving. Have you ever seen Ginger get rid of a strange dog that comes into our yard? She just keeps walking with the dog to the edge of the property, sort of a 'Here's your hat, what's your hurry' attitude. Then, if the dog moves back toward the house, she sits down—so she's between the strange dog and our house—so the dog would have to go past her to get back to the house."

Gaia loves her dogs. She sleeps with them next to her bed, notices their characteristics, draws pictures of them, and writes about them. The first book she made was about her dogs. "Ginger is sweet and she has brains," she had written in that first book.

Ginger can talk, we have both noticed. Ginger can say, "Where were you?" in a way that is distinctly clear. We think Ginger is teaching Crusher to talk. Crusher tries hard, but her sounds are unintelligible. Crusher pulls at the end of the leash; I can see every muscle in her body ripple.

The sky is streaked with gold, pink, amber, rose. Here the water is a metallic pink and blue, like colors painted on a mirror. Gaia is delighted with the way the blue of the sky and the gold of the setting sun are marbleized in the water and with the way the colors keep changing with the changing light.

It is almost dark when we go back and climb into the high, old metal bed and invite the dogs to curl up beside it. Gaia and I get out our respective books to read, but first we read together. We have been reading out loud to each other at night for years—ever since she learned how to read—and we take turns with whatever book it is.

We read everything that comes along that seems interesting and well written, regardless of whether or not the book is for children or adults, obscure or a classic. We read for enjoyment and for information. We read because we love the sound of each other's voice. And we read because we like to know how the other reacts to the same thing.

On this trip it's been "The Voyage of the Dawn Treader," and soon we are both nodding off over, "The wind never failed, but grew gentler every day til at length the waves were little more than ripples."

Both dogs are asleep now, Ginger under the bed and Crusher next to it. I carefully move Gaia's reading book and set it on the stand next to the bed. Then I get up and walk across the cold floor to the light switch and then make my way back in the dark. Gradually I fall asleep to the unfamiliar creaks and moans of the cabin settling around us in the dark.

At midnight, it must be, or thereabouts, I hear Crusher roaming the cabin like a caged animal. Afraid first that there's an animal outside—skunk, maybe; bear, unlikely—and then, concerned that the dog has to go to the bathroom, I finally make myself get up to see what she needs. I throw my down jacket over my nightgown and slip into moccasins and head outside with her, leaving Ginger for Gaia's protection and comfort.

It is pitch-black under the trees outside the cabin. Ahead of me for five hundred feet or so it is so dark under the tall elms and maples that I can only sense my way in the dark. I move toward the trail that winds through the cabin court, where the gibbous moon shining down from very high above creates a glittery, sharp, white light just above the narrow road.

How dark and quiet the night is. How cold and clear. Even the lake is quiet. I strain to hear the water lapping at the shore, but nothing. There are no insects, no night birds, no frog sounds. I move toward the lake, wanting to get out to where I can see more stars. I stand for a moment where I can now hear, faintly, the water sound.

The water that encircles this island touches at some time everywhere. *We are all everything and connected somehow in spirit and in fact,* I am thinking as I hear the sound of the water. Somewhere thousands of miles south of us this water is touching a tropical island; somewhere only a few hundred miles north of here, it is the edge of near-ice.

I do not stray too far from the cabin because of Gaia sleeping there. I had wanted her to see a whole island of people with dark eyes and dark skin and ways of moving and thinking like hers. It was to have been one of those quiet gifts a mother gives a child. But it didn't happen.

Other than some people in their cars on the ferry who may or may not have been of Algonquian ancestry, we have not seen a single Native American on this island since we arrived. Not in the stores, not in the resorts. They *were* here. For fifty centuries my daughter's ancestors on her father's side seasonally camped on the St. Marys River, made maple syrup, fished the rapids, raised their children. Now I think there must be very few, or where are they?

I am freezing and feel in my pocket for a cigarette. I find a crumpled pack of Marlboros and pull one out. Gaia lectures me on smoking, so I sneak cigarettes late at night, like a teenager. It glows orange in the dark. Although I have no more sense of where I am—other than being on some ancient river island between Canada and the United States halfway between the West Coast and the East Coast—I feel oddly at peace.

I walk slowly up and down the gravel and moss two-track. There is frost on the gravel, frost on the moss. It is icy cold;

dark, but clear. A night for dogs to call, but no dogs do. After a few minutes I return with Crusher to the cabin.

At 4 A.M. Gaia cries out in her sleep. I wake abruptly, feeling lost in dreams, and rise and wander through the cabin, sweeping shadows before me. The moon has gone down.

I am uneasy, my mind beleaguered by nightmare thoughts, dim images, grim details from the news on TV in the motel we stayed at, the cheery voice of the lady on "Good Morning America," talking about the movie, *Batman;* the bulletins broadcast at 6 A.M., the unnamed faces of the war dead, the views and facts of the news hideously intertwined with ads for toys and cars. Enticements to buy sugary cereals in pretty boxes and advertisements for fancy, shiny cars driven by well-heeled men and women on vacation are bizarrely interspersed with grisly accounts of heinous crimes—Jeffrey Dahmer capturing and eating children while the screams of the victims go unreported, or when reported, ignored by the police.

In the early 1990s American television viewers and radio listeners are daily treated to these daunting truths: a person is murdered every thirty-six hours in Oakland; one-fourth of America's children live in poverty; this four-billion-year-old earth currently loses three animal species a day. What is in the future for us all?

In the present, at least, in Gaia's and my life at home, there is no TV. We have never had one, so the only TV Gaia gets to watch is at her friends' houses or in motel rooms. I know this is part of my attempt to sweeten reality for her, in effect lie to her, make up the world, paint a happier picture, in order to prolong her innocence, which I see as so quickly passing, with the hope that she will be able to be a child long enough to grow up. But there is so much I can't protect her from. Some of the most insidious things are unconsciously taught to children in our schools. I see her do her homework, learning about Indians and Pilgrims and the first Thanksgiving. Do they really think the Indians are thankful the Pilgrims came?

If Native Americans are mentioned in her history books, it

is as people who probably migrated across the Bering Sea, a conquering culture's self-serving view of things, implying that since we are all in essence immigrants, we all have an equal right to be here. Maybe Native Americans did come across the Bering Sea, but what if it is discovered that the footprints were going the other way?

We sleep until the sunlight is flooding the bedroom. Gaia wakes singing the theme song from the movie, *Lean on Me*. Breakfast is peanuts and more grapefruit juice and Fig Newtons, then a long walk and church at St. Luke's on the Trail. Here are mainly retired people, at this time of year, welcoming and kind but singing of sin and repentance. We actually sing, until I'm giddy, "Onward Christian soldiers, marching as to war, with the cross of Jesus, going on before." My voice cracks on Jesus and Gaia looks up at me, rolling her eyes warningly. It's been years since I've been inside a Christian church. I'd forgotten what it was like, and the emphasis on sin comes as a shock to me.

Afterward we stand on the porch of the church, a knotty pine church they have all built themselves, a church like a Viking ship, and these people like the ancestors of the Vikings, all white people, eating cake and drinking coffee and asking me where I'm from and I'm so nervous all I can talk about is what a great island this would be for smuggling.

"Mom," Gaia says the minute we're in the car and driving out the bumpy gravel road, "was all you could think of to talk about *smuggling*? 'You could smuggle by boat, you could smuggle by plane.' The way they were looking at you!"

Pauline and Ed Andrews's house, a white frame house on the way to the ferry, is set back in dark evergreens. I am surprised to see that Pauline and Ed Andrews are Native American and they may be equally surprised to see that Gaia is, but none of us let on. We head back into the woods along a trail. We leave Ginger in the car and take Crusher with us.

The dark trees here are thick, tight, and in places where they are very tall there is a clear, almost swept-looking, pine needle-covered forest floor. Duck Island is an island in a lake on Sugar Island.

Everything here—and perhaps everything in the whole St. Marys River archipelago, is like a wilderness Venice, a labyrinth of land and water, where there are islands within lakes within islands within lakes, where rivers become lakes and lakes become rivers and become lakes again.

Crusher amuses Ed because she follows so obediently beside us, never racing off into the woods after squirrels or rabbits. He says if I ever want to give Crusher away I can give her to him. The Andrews maintain this place for the University of Michigan, which now uses it as a base for biological research.

The entire area was once the summer home and hunting camp of Chase Salmon Osborn, governor of Michigan in 1911. Born to a poor pioneer family in Indiana in 1860, Osborn went to Purdue University when he was fourteen. He discovered iron ore in Michigan in his early twenties and amassed an immense fortune.

It is warm in the sun, cool in the shade. We come to a little trestle bridge over a waterway. Pauline points to a spot where Mr. Osborn had planted water lilies. Here the well-worn path goes up over rocks, through an area of berry bushes and ground pine, to a clearing with an ancient log cabin in it.

"This was Little Duck," Pauline says, nodding her head toward the crumbling cabin. "It will have to be torn down soon. They already took down part of it. It was rotten." Pauline and Ed's relative, a man by the name of Gib, had been Governor Osborn's personal guide and all-around caretaker. The name Gib, they tell us, means "he who sits easy."

Around in back of the decrepit cabin is a strange framework, about six feet long and four feet high, narrow as a bier, rimmed with rocks, filled with dead boughs. "This was Governor Osborn's bed," Pauline says. "He slept outside on these evergreen boughs."

Governor Osborn, Pauline tells us, believed if he slept with his head to the north, he could take advantage of the earth's natural magnetism, that the ions would line up in his body, north to south, and that he would be healthier as a result, and stronger. He lived to be one hundred-and-one years old, so maybe he was right.

The governor died years ago, but someone has replaced these boughs as recently as perhaps last summer. I assume they must give impromptu tours here and have kept this filled to show people. I touch one.

"Balsam," Pauline says. "That's good for arthritis. That's an Indian cure. You put that in the sweat lodge, or the sauna, that helps with arthritis. That's true."

We move on through the woods. Finally we reach a large concrete structure that resembles a dungeon but that Pauline says is the library. She takes me into a place filled with old, moldering documents.

Here is an old fireplace that hasn't been used in years. Old copies of books, reprints of pamphlets and magazine articles are everywhere in a kind of disarray, as though someone had been hastily packing and had been interrupted midway.

She hands me a gray-blue pamphlet, *First Inaugural Message* of Governor Chase Salmon Osborn. "He was only governor for a term," she says. "I guess he got bored."

She says this indifferently, and I turn and look at Ed to see if the expression on his face will reveal amusement or something else at Pauline's remark, but he is showing Gaia lumps of iron ore Governor Osborn found. I move up and down the table. Many of the articles are by Chase Salmon Osborn and Stellanova Osborn. I comment on the unusualness of the name Stellanova and Pauline says, "His adopted daughter. He came to give a speech at the college where she was at and they just took to each other."

"Did he have other children?"

Pauline shrugs. "He had a wife, and children. On his deathbed, Stellanova married him."

"Why?"

"When she married him, he was in a coma," Pauline says.

"She had all these lawyers there." I don't know how to pursue this. I'm thinking of the bed of balsam boughs.

Here, inside the old library, I learn that Chase Osborn, known as the Iron Hunter for his discoveries of iron ore in the Upper Peninsula and Canada, has written a book by that name where he writes that he found "a home for life" on Sugar Island. This wilderness, he writes, drew him like a "human lodestone."

Sculptor Carleton W. Angell came to Sugar Island to do a bust of Osborn in the 1930s and relates that he had scarcely met the man, when Osborn abruptly "excused himself, saying that he was right in the midst of looking up something pertaining to the human gullet or esophagus." Osborn hurried away and then returned to his guest and thereupon "recited a lengthy account of the Angell family in America, going all the way back to Thomas Angell in Boston in 1631." There were other exchanges, too, that revealed Osborn as a man of supreme self-confidence and eccentricity.

Osborn had a surprisingly mystical turn of mind. In an essay entitled "The Law of Divine Concord—an Ozark Revelation" he writes, "I clambered up and down the throbbing hills of the Ozarks and got lost with God. God is life. God is consciousness. God and Life and Consciousness are One. Since the beginning there has been the contest between the thing called death and the thing called life. But death is only the wrecking of a broken tenement to make way for a better one; it is progress." He writes that he preferred to pray to God the Mother instead of God the Father because the Christian notion of God grew out of a time "when the masculine was everything," and that time was passing. I'm struck by what an unusual view that must have been for the early 1900s and how much more often one hears that sentiment in our times. I feel uncomfortably like a voyeur, here among the governor's papers. I cast a sidelong glance at Pauline.

"He was a genius," she says good-naturedly, shrugging, as if sensing my discomfiture and encouraging me to continue perusing.

I sit for a minute at the long library table and skim at random Governor Osborn's inaugural speech, where he has addressed no fewer than forty-seven issues. An environmentalist ahead of his time, he thought trees should be replaced as they were cut.

In his short tenure as governor, Osborn passed the first workman's compensation act. He was concerned with the rights of the common, working people, whom he saw as the backbone of democracy and whose rights and ability to feed themselves and their families therefore had to be protected by the government. He spoke against a society motivated by the need for material goods. "There is enough to go around," he wrote, "if all would take only their fair share."

Gaia is politely going around the room with Ed Andrews. "He built this here because he was afraid of fire," Pauline says of the library room we're in. She hands me a giant four-page photo feature from the *Detroit Free Press* in 1941 showing the Governor at Possum Poke, his Georgia plantation, complete with many black servants smiling toothily. There are photos of the "fabulous" Governor and Miss Stellanova Osborn, his "adopted daughter and associate-secretary-critic" inspecting the apple blossoms. Here is a photo of the eighty-one-year-old Governor doing his morning exercises, here is another of him dictating a letter to Stellanova.

What was his view of women? Of African Americans? Of Native Americans? He had plenty of people of color waiting on him—servants, caretakers, fire makers, food preparers, bed makers. Did he send any of these people to college? Did he buy them books? How did his wife feel about Stellanova? Was Stellanova called Stellanova before he met her or did he, in his ardor, name her that? Did he really consider Stellanova his adopted daughter or was this what in poetry is called a conceit, or fanciful notion? Did Stellanova feel like a concubine all those years and is that why she finessed a legal marriage with him while the old coot lay dying? I can't even think *Stellanova,* much less say it, without feeling hoodwinked.

The room we're in is cold and damp, as if it's been shut up a long time. It has high, fifteen-foot ceilings and two small windows. It appears to have thick concrete walls. Crusher is in the room, checking things out, too, but she does not harm things and anyway things look as though they've been neglected here for a very long time. Crusher finally satisfies her nose for new scents and curls up on a threadbare old sisal rug.

"You're nice and quiet," Ed says in his sweet, slightly sing-song way, to no one in particular, "just like your dog. Maybe you could go find a nice rug to lie down on."

I'm taken aback by this remark and can't figure out who it's addressed to; then I realize he's talking to Gaia. I don't let on, but out of the corner of my eye I try to see what Gaia's reaction is. She looks as noncommittal as Ed and a polite smile plays across her face for a moment, like a ray of sunlight in this dark, damp fortress of a former library.

Then we move outside, into the dew-drenched, shady clearing. There is a feeling here by Osborn's blockhouse library that is cloying, that I want to escape.

I move into the sunlight near the lake but I can't shake off the feeling of wanting to get back to my car, and after a minute I figure out what it is that bothers me. It feels like a time warp of the early 1900s that I can't totally inhabit or understand and so, like a dress that doesn't fit, I want to get out of it.

"They're going to burn it down," Pauline says. She has an unusual way of talking, that is both staccato and low-pitched. She turns and looks at the old building. "I'm going to have to move into Sault Ste. Marie with my daughter. I can't afford to live here. It costs too much to go back and forth to work on the ferry. Then there will be no one to take care of it."

I don't ask, but I imagine her existence, tied as it was to Osborn's hunting camp through her relative, is precarious now that Gib is gone and she will be hard-pressed to find any way to make a living on Sugar Island.

We walk down to the shore in front of the library and then around to the back. We are all here for such a brief time, I am thinking, even a five-thousand-year tenure for the Algonquian tribes is nothing, for now they have all virtually vanished from this island.

And it isn't just these tribes who are disappearing: that would be the short view. Blue-eyed people like myself are a mere 3 percent of the global population. In another fifty years, Caucasians generally will make up only 9 percent of the global population. Certainly in another five thousand years, and maybe in only a couple of hundred, we ourselves will be a dim memory, like the hairy, beetle-browed Neanderthals who some say became incorporated into fairy tales as trolls, we will become characters of folklore. Our great-great-great-great-great-great-great-great-great-great grandchildren will tell stories about the people with white skin and red hair who lived once upon a time in a mythic former world, as unimaginable to our future progeny as the worlds of five thousand years ago, or even fifty, are to us.

I feel layers of lives all around me in my mind. I want to banish not just the duality of body and soul, the dichotomy of life and death, which Osborn wrote about in his Ozark vision, but banish time. I can't imagine his life on Sugar Island fifty years ago, let alone the eons that rolled by before that. More than we are all ethnocentric, we are timecentric. Periods of history, much less prehistory, that we are not part of and cannot witness personally, can never be fully comprehended. Even when we know everything there is to know, we cannot know, because we were not there.

I am amazed to come upon the crumbling ruins of this former Michigan governor's summer camp in this remote and forgotten pocket of the American continent. It confounds the senses to picture a man of Osborn's towering mind and eccentricity as a Michigan governor, although the very thought presents a refreshing change from the steady succession of bland and smugly anti-intellectual governors of today.

Suddenly I recall something I'd read in Alexis de Tocqueville's journals about his visit to America in 1831. He wanted to get to Michigan, the real frontier, to outdistance what he called, "the European hordes," the people who had populated this new and wild land. He makes it to Pontiac, then nothing but wilderness, with a companion. It is near nightfall.

They need to change horses. Someone sends them out to a log cabin in the woods. It is summer and there's a full moon, so they keep walking. They finally come to this house where there's "an excellent bed" in one corner and a woman in it "dressed like a lady." Tocqueville is nonplussed, as well he might be. "Strange mixture of prosperity and poverty," he scrawls in his notebook. "The Americans in their log houses have the air of rich folk who have temporarily gone to spend a season in a hunting-lodge."

There is a dual quality about Osborn's camp that is at one and the same time, as Tocqueville observed about his Americans, like an aristocrat playing at camping, but also, like a camper playing at being an aristocrat.

We go back a different way than we came, along a ridge above another inlet. "This big rock," Ed says, pointing to a rock in the bank, "the governor had it moved here. It cracked. It was a spirit rock. It should have never been moved. It brought bad luck. That's when he started losing all his money."

Gaia and I are in the car and headed out the bumpy gravel road toward the ferry, before we both turn and look at each other and start laughing. "When he said about the dog," I blurt out. "What did he say again?"

Gaia smiles and shakes her head from side to side, repeating what he had said, "'You're nice and quiet, just like the dog, maybe you could go find a nice rug to lie down on.'"

We both laugh.

"Was he trying to get a reaction?"

"Well, if he was trying to get a reaction," Gaia says, "he didn't."

The September afternoon sun is summer bright, hot on my skin as it shines through the car window, but the quality of the light everywhere outside is late autumn, with those large, barely visible, gently moving, Caspar-the-Ghost-shaped, paisley pieces of light wafting here and there on the air.

The ferry is waiting at the river and we are the second-to-last car hustled on before the metal gates at the back of the boat clank shut and are bolted by the athletic ferryman.

I see Gaia dropping sunflower seeds to Reepicheep and think, a mouse once named can never be just a mouse again. "Life is so short," I say to her, glancing at where she has dropped the seeds, "might as well be nice to mice. Nothing else for it: we'll have to keep Reepicheep. At least for the trip home."

I look to the fields and the woods, to the shadows of the trees across the road, the shadows of the dark junipers in the dead meadows, shadows that are long and have a purplish cast. It will be dusk before we are home in Leelanau.

I picture the routines of my life in my old farmhouse on the Leelanau, and the daily life there, even with all its flawed humanness and boring ordinariness, seems suddenly much more acceptable than it did even a week ago. The thought of being home, feeding the animals, calling my neighbors, getting Gaia ready for school in the morning, seems comforting, like a lamp in a window on a dark night.

Michigan's Oldest
Living Synagogue

On a little back street in Traverse City, tucked in among larger, more modern buildings, is a tiny, old Jewish synagogue. It is the oldest Jewish synagogue in continuous use in Michigan. It is old enough to have had the land for it donated by an early lumber baron, old enough to have been built on the town's Boardman River when mostly Native Americans navigated that river, and when everything beyond Traverse City was a trackless wilderness.

I visited there one late autumn evening when the geese were going "wonka, wonka, wonka" south and the light was driving through the cloud cover in Rembrandt-like shafts, and thought about the temple, which looks like an old, one-room schoolhouse, and thought about how for Jewish people in the 1890s the temple represented tradition in the midst of frontier transience.

But for Jewish people in the 1990s, it probably represents tradition in the midst of a different kind of frontier transience— the frontier of the almost unfathomable global changes that we all contend with daily.

I don't know that I want to be Jewish specifically, or that it would be possible even if I did, but I would like to belong to some tribe or group. I have always envied Jewish people their automatic tribalism, their sense of connectedness to each other and to more than five thousand years of shared history. My family, what I know of it, came to this country three hundred years ago and married anybody who happened to get off the boat after that. If I ever had a tribe it was probably the Visigoths.

So like a beggar at a feast, I ended up at Temple Beth El during Simchas Torah, a holiday which, loosely translated, means "Happy Torah." There are readings like "Torah—The Elixir of Jewish Life," with lines like, "Toil not merely for worldly goods, find time also for study of the Torah. For if you lack knowledge, what have you acquired? If you have acquired knowledge, what do you lack?"

This is the day the final portion of the year's reading of the Torah is completed, the entire Torah unscrolled and rolled back up again. It is cold this night in October and there are bright stars overhead as I follow the congregation out one door of the temple and in another. Children carry apples on flags and the sweet smell of the apples is sharp on the night air. All the people—children and adults—sing and dance around the outside of the temple, then back in again, then out again, following the Torahs, which are carried aloft by their rabbi and another member of the synagogue.

There are perhaps thirty people here this night, all in a festive and gentle mood. After the services there are refreshments downstairs: coffee and tea for the grownups, cookies and apple juice for the children. Here is Wesley Odell, the visiting rabbi from Hebrew Union College in Cincinnati, holding a new baby. Here is Terry Tarnow, fixing a young child's apple on a flag.

For the first time in nearly a century, the temple has a growing congregation instead of a dwindling one. By the early 1900s, the Jewish families who had built the temple had, by and large, left for places like Detroit, where, according to a booklet on the synagogue, "a large Jewish community had more to offer their marriageable sons and daughters."

Mickey Fivenson, a well-known Traverse city businessman and civic leader, remembers growing up in Traverse City in the

1950s and being one of the only Jewish students in the Traverse City school system. There was no prejudice that he recalls, but also no awareness of his religion. Every year he was given a part in the school Christmas play, with no one but him understanding how odd that was.

Now Jewish families are moving back to Traverse City, they tell me, drawn by the good schools, clean water, clean air, and safe streets. They have come to Traverse City because, in a changing and increasingly violent world, this is a good place to raise children. The synagogue has again become the center of social and religious life that it was created for when Traverse City was a lumber boom town, a place for them to connect to each other and to their history.

But no one at Temple Beth El, including Fivenson, makes the claim that Traverse City is anything but an outpost. "The reality is that we only have a rabbi twice a month [and for ten weeks in the summer]," says congregation member Lois Kowalski, a former New Yorker now on the staff at Interlochen Arts Academy. "We fly him in from Cincinnati once or twice a month and that's as often as we can afford to do it. There isn't any access to Jewish food here, or Jewish books or culture. My kids were, for years, the only Jewish kids in their school."

So how do people who have managed to maintain Jewish culture in all parts of the world for the last 5,753 years do it in Traverse City? The answer is, with a lot of flexibility and tenacity, and with a lot of mixed marriages. More than 40 percent of the couples who attend Temple Beth El, according to several estimates, are couples where one person has converted to Judaism. Obviously the alternative was to go back to Detroit as the first settlers had done, and the newcomers to Traverse City aren't doing that.

Adaptability is evident in other areas as well. Because there are no kosher butchers in Traverse City, some of the synagogue members have skirted the dietary laws by becoming vegetarian.

Some issues, however, are not so easily resolved. One area of controversy a few years ago centered around a key, money-making effort. Temple Beth El paid for its rabbi primarily through a highly successful Christmas gift-wrapping booth at the Cherryland Mall. Aside from the issue of making money off Christmas, a more critical issue for religious traditionalists was that the booth should not be operated on the Sabbath—from Friday night through Saturday—some of the best gift-wrapping business hours.

The gift-wrapping may not have been of deep philosophical or religious significance, but it is at the heart of the question of how much *can* a group change, and how much *should* it change if it is going to maintain its identity.

Jeff Green, a Traverse City attorney at that time and member of the congregation during the gift-wrapping controversy, is in many ways an example of both the assimilation that takes place in America, not just among Jewish people but all people, and the ambivalence about that assimilation.

In almost a prose-poem of ambivalence, Green, who was single then, talked about marriage. "There aren't very many Jewish women in Traverse City," he said, "so I don't date Jewish women, although I don't know that I would anyway. If I were married to a Jewish woman, I know I would probably be more involved in the temple. But I don't know that I would actively seek a Jewish woman. I know I wouldn't want to raise my kids as Christians." Green eventually moved back to the more metropolitan area of Lansing, but many more have come to replace him.

Today many of those who attend Temple Beth El are young newlyweds. Lana and Harley Sherman recently moved to Traverse City and Lana, an enthusiastic convert to Judaism, says, "I love it here. I like the beaches. The synagogue has done more than a lot to make us welcome."

"The congregation at Temple Beth El is very family oriented," Sherman says. "When we had our baby, everyone was ready to help us. Wesley Odell, the student rabbi, is so down-to-earth. He's my age. He's like the brother I never had. I never had a religion growing up. Now I do. It's a good feeling. My father passed away when I was pregnant with Josh. Before, I just thought when you died you were buried.

Now I know my father's in Heaven, and he can see Josh whenever he wants."

Susan Abrahams moved to Traverse City a few years ago from Long Island. She has two toddlers, Jacob and Robbie. She was managing her family's retail business in northern Michigan when through her work, she met her husband, Randy Hansen. "He's not Jewish, but he's very supportive. He always wanted to raise his children in a religion."

Susan says she misses her family, but the congregation of Temple Beth El has helped her adjust. "This is a very close-knit, supportive group. There are people in it who aren't Jewish and they are made to feel welcome, too."

Three months later, both of these young mothers are at Jennie Belfour's a few blocks away on Oak Street, visiting. "Call me Jennie," Mrs. Belfour says the minute she opens the door, and a minute later, "have a cookie."

Mrs. Belfour is "everyone's grandmother," Susan Abrahams says. She is the oldest member of the Temple Beth El congregation, and because she cannot get out easily, the members of the congregation come to her. In addition to the young mothers visiting her during the daytime, she says, young men from the congregation come by after work and on weekends to shovel her walk or take her grocery shopping.

"I came to this country in 1920, when I was fifteen," Mrs. Belfour says. "Now you know how old I am. We had discrimination in Russia, yes. Only 10 percent of the Jewish children could go to school. There was the First World War, then there was the Revolution. After the Revolution it was everyone took over. We had the cossacks for a couple of weeks. We had the Germans for two days. Then the Polish soldiers came in.

"There were many Polish soldiers. They put two in our house. One of them got fresh with my older sister. She slapped him. In the middle of the night she went to Warsaw. She got in touch with my father—in America. From Russia during the war there had been no way to reach him, but now the war was over. We left everything. Furniture, of course. Everything. We came to America."

Younger members of the congregation like Susan Abrahams and Lana Sherman visit Mrs. Belfour for her, and for themselves. "I visit Jennie Belfour mostly because she's lonely and I think it makes a brightness in her day," Susan Abrahams says, "although lately my kids have been so wild I don't know that it does. And I visit her for me. My mother is far away. My children don't have a grandmother nearby, so Jennie is that grandmother for them. She's their link to what went before. That accent, they'll never hear again."

The people coming to visit Jennie Belfour remind me of people I've seen on islands. They reach out, they check on each other, they visit and share stories and cookies. Temple Beth El is a version of an island society, and, with all its flexibility and ability to adapt to the times, it is an island of "unchange" in a sea of change.

Ellen Fivenson is visiting Jennie. Originally from the Detroit area, Ellen says she and Jennie both moved to Traverse City in the 1970s. "We were like a family," Jennie says. "We just clicked." Ellen nods.

"I can't believe Julius is gone," Jennie Belfour says, trying to keep herself from choking up as she speaks. "Sixty-six and a half years we were married and it seems like yesterday I met him." Julius Belfour died recently and this steady stream of visitors helps keep Jennie company and helps her adjust to her husband's absence.

C. S. Lewis in *A Grief Observed* writes that he dreaded being alone after his wife died, although when he was with people he didn't want to talk to them. He just liked having them around him. Jennie says something of the same and several times she mentions that she has become forgetful since Julius died. "I go into a room to get something, and I forget what it is. I used to remember *everything,* now I remember *nothing.*"

Ellen reaches across the dining room table and pats Jennie's arm. "You miss having someone to *kvetch* with," she says. How do they know to do this, I wonder, how do they know to visit each other? They must have seen their mothers do it.

Jennie takes a gilt-framed picture of a young couple dressed in the style of the 1940s down off the shelf. "Look," she says. "This is when we were first married. I was tall then," she says. I look at her, an ancient lady, four feet tall, or less. "I shrank," she says, putting the picture back.

Lois Kowalski visits, coming in the kitchen door, stomping snow off her boots, telling Jennie she can just stop for a minute because she's on her way to pick up her son. Jennie is making an afghan for Lois's college-aged daughter. "I think more red around the border," she says and Lois holds it up to look and agrees. "Yes, that would be nice. More red."

Together we figure out how old their religion is. If Christianity will be 2,000 years old in eight years, then the Jewish religion is 5,753 years old, or is it 5,752 years old? "It was before Solomon built the temple," Jennie says. "And before Moses," I add. Later I call Wesley Odell, who is making his bimonthly visit to the Temple Beth El congregation for the weekend of January 24, 1992, and he confirms it: the Jewish religion has been around 5,752 years.

All the people visiting Jennie Belfour sustain each other. The young women keep Jennie from being lonely, keep her busy, and keep her and themselves connected to the past and the present. This is no small thing in an America where half the people move every four years. This temple is a living network of friends and congregation members who consciously, but unpretentiously, entertain and comfort each other.

Leaving Jennie Belfour's house on Oak Street for the last time on a bitterly cold day, I decide to drive down Washington Street toward Temple Beth El. I take the remnant of South Park Street along beside the large, old Jacobson stone Bethany Baptist Church, in past the large, new modern jail, past the huge windowless edifice of the new city-county building complex to the east, into the large, bleak parking lot where tiny, homey, shiplap-sided Temple Beth El, with its Star of David, remains exactly as it was when it was built in 1885 on the banks of this Boardman River.

It is one of those sunny cold days, warm out of the wind, almost hot inside my car, and I sit there for a minute basking in the heat and the sunshine, drinking the last of a flat Diet Coke that has been in my car since that morning. After a minute or two, I get out and go up the steps to the synagogue. It is locked and so I just stand there for a moment, half-dazed from the sunlight, looking at a piece of ornate brass, roughly the size of a Tootsie Roll, attached to the door frame. I recognize this from my years of living in New York City in the 1970s and seeing them on the doors of friends' apartments, but I can't remember the name of it. Menorah? No, that's for candles. Finally it comes to me: mezuzah. Something about doors or gates. I think of this tiny temple's humble doorpost hosting a tradition that goes back more than 5,000 years in a town that, in the long view, is barely settled.

I walk back down the cobblestone steps of the synagogue. On one side of the steps there is a large cement urn with frost-blackened geraniums in it and next to it, a marvelously small, baby tennis shoe. Someone found it, I am thinking, and put it there, hoping whoever lost it would see it.

I walk toward the Boardman River and then make my way down the bank where an ancient, big-trunked willow seems to offer shelter. I sit down and watch the play of sunlight and shadow on the opposite bank and see in my mind again the baby tennis shoe and then my mind shifts to the many-acred, huge, new Dayton-Hudson Mall on the hills above Traverse City.

I am thinking about the balance between the old and the new, the light and the dark, the spirit and the body. I am thinking about all of human history as a never-ending play of light and shadow down through the ages. I recall something Ellen Fivenson said, "If you want to keep and hold certain principles, certain traditions, you have to make some adaptations, but the whole point is to keep those traditions. Because that's what life is about, the weaving together of all those elements—the religious traditions with that everyday sense of who you are."

All other things being equal, as I sit on the banks of the Boardman River on a sunny, cold day, near Temple Beth El and near a slew of construction trailers, counting the birds' nests left in the bare branches like so many snagged mittens—I think there will, in a hundred years, be a Boardman River, and I think there will also be a Temple Beth El. Perhaps no longer an outpost.

The Deer

A few years ago, on the first day of hunting season, I was driving my youngest daughter home from kindergarten and a deer rushed down off the hill and into the path of our car.

The deer was being chased by hunters and was not looking where it was going. I swerved to avoid it, then curved my body over Gaia's in the seat next to me, to protect her if the deer came through the windshield.

The next thing I heard was a terrible thud and I looked up to see that the deer had collided with the back end of our car. The deer lay on the highway, dazed. After a moment or two, it started to move. It was not dead, as it turns out, only maimed. Its hindquarters appeared to have been broken, but its front legs were still good.

As hunters and other motorists and spectators gathered, the deer—the whites of its eyes showing—frantically pulled itself around the wet highway by its front legs. It was terribly wounded and terribly alive. It was a doe. We were within inches of her and could see her face clearly.

We watched her, paralyzed, for what seemed like an eternity. Not one of the hunters raised his gun to shoot her, although many were armed. Finally, a hunter who had figured out a way to kill her without using up the hunting license he had paid for came forward and knifed her in the neck.

Shortly after we arrived home, a policeman came to take

down the details of the incident and make out an accident report. After he left I realized my daughter was nowhere around. I looked all through the house for her and, not finding her, went out into the yard and began calling for her. After a moment or two I heard the cedar tree rustling and saw her climbing down. This is a giant cedar, with thick foliage, and one need only climb up inside it to disappear.

I asked her if she was upset about the policeman or the deer.

She said it was the deer.

I told her the hunters were hunting for food for their families, and that this was a normal part of life. I know that food is not the only reason hunters hunt but atavism and bloodlust are too complex for me to understand, let alone explain, so I left it at food.

She asked if we ate deer. I answered that we did. Then she said, "I will never eat deer."

Her vegetarianism was a progression from there. First she wouldn't eat venison, then she wouldn't eat anything that looked like venison. Then she stopped eating hot dogs, chicken, and fish.

This child is now twelve and has been strictly vegetarian for seven years. The other day, shopping with her at Oryana, our vegetarian food store, I asked her if she remembered the time we hit the deer, or the time the deer hit us, and the day the policeman came and she hid in the cedar tree. She said she didn't remember the deer or the policeman. She did remember hiding in the cedar tree.

She smiled at me. "I must have repressed it."

I smiled, too, and didn't say anything. Later that day I thought about this as I was about to take a load of wet wash out to hang it on the line.

I did this and while walking across the lawn, and while noticing the tiger lilies in bloom around the base of that gigantic cedar tree, and while watching the pair of cardinals in the birch tree and while hanging the wash—half-mesmerized by the familiar rhythms of something I had done all my life—I wondered how many versions of how many forgotten deer are at work in the psyches of all of us, as we go about our daily tasks, choosing to do one thing instead of another, unremembering but determined.

Pygmalion on the Frontier

One of the most puzzling marriages in Michigan history, perhaps in American history, has to have been that between Henry Schoolcraft and his Native American wife, Jane. Henry, whose name now graces roads, schools, and counties in Michigan, was an explorer who worked for the United States Department of War. He was the Indian agent at Sault Ste. Marie from 1823 to 1833. Jane was the daughter of an aristocratic Irish fur trader, John Johnston, and his wife, Ozhaw-Guscoday-Wayquay, daughter of a powerful Chippewa chief.

Trying to imagine the Schoolcraft marriage is like trying to imagine Pygmalion married to Galatea, because like Pygmalion, Schoolcraft fashioned Jane after his idea of what she should be; and like Galatea, Jane was mysterious and silent.

The two of them met at a sugaring-off party in Sault Ste. Marie in 1822 and were married in 1823. Henry was thirty. Jane was twenty-three. Jane had been educated in Ireland by wealthy aunts and, by frontier standards, must have been something of a hothouse flower. Henry, who we are told had no interest in women until he met Jane, had been traveling around the interior of the country for years, sitting on the bottom of a canoe, taking notes, and was ready, as he said, for the blandishments of domestic life.

Jane's family was the most powerful family at the Soo. "Naturally," writes Mentor L. Williams, editor of Schoolcraft's journals, "their connections with the Indians afforded an opportunity Schoolcraft could not neglect."

[99]

Jane is described in the correspondence of the period as a great beauty. Thomas McKenney, a Washington official who visited the Soo, described Jane in a letter to his wife. "Mildness of expression, and softness, and delicacy of manner as well as of voice, characterize her," he wrote. "You would never judge, either from her complexion or her language, that her mother was Chippewa."

Around this time Henry wrote a poem entitled "The Choice," dedicated to Miss J. J., wherein he congratulates himself on finding in her the retiring nature that qualifies her to be his bride: a person of "sweet, retiring, simple, modest mien . . . in virtue principled, in manners guarded; kind to all others in a just degree, but fixed, devoted, loving only me."

Initially, perhaps as in all marriages, the Schoolcraft union seems to have been happy, and they appear to have succeeded in carving out a personal and even intellectual life for themselves amidst the chaos of the frontier. Henry engaged Jane in writing for his magazine, *The Literary Voyager*. In a coy address to the readers, he writes, "The letters of our female correspondent 'Leelinau,' we have pursued with pleasure, and recommend to the attention of our readers. Her lines under 'Rosa,' possess chasteness in the selection of her imagines, united to a pleasing versification." For himself, he took the names Damoetas and Ekedo. They worked together researching and compiling Indian legends.

Two of the accomplishments Henry Schoolcraft is most famous for occurred during the early years of his marriage to Jane and were the direct result of her assistance and connections. The first was the researching of many Chippewa legends, including those that became the basis of Longfellow's *Hiawatha*. The second was the discovery of the source of the Mississippi. It is unlikely that either of these achievements would have been possible for him without her.

On 27 June 1824, a son, William Henry, was born: "a beautiful, bright-eyed little stranger," Henry Schoolcraft writes, "with a face of the purest Caucasian whiteness." He must have loved this firstborn child. He writes tenderly of how his son "played with his shadow as a phenomenon... [and] talked to his dog as if it possessed reason." Soon after, Schoolcraft began planning to build his home at Elmwood, at the Soo where the river would "run majestically before our doors."

But after that, something went sour. In 1827, William Henry died suddenly of the croup just before he turned three. The Schoolcrafts appear to have been overcome with grief. They moved out of the home where the child had died—leaving the furniture still standing—and moved in with Jane's parents until fall. Eventually, under their own roof again, two more children were born, Janee in 1828 and Johnston in 1829, but the marriage seems to have suffered a permanent blow from which it could never recover.

During these years, Schoolcraft was gone constantly in his work, assaying Indian lands and converting them to the United States domain. Jane is reported as increasingly ill, her undiagnosed pain, according to one source, treated with morphine.

We never learn the nature of Jane's sickness. She is variously described as "living in her bed," and "appearing with damp, tremulous hands," to greet visitors. Schoolcraft's second wife, who presumably got her information from Henry, will tell us Jane's illness was simply a fiendish addiction to opium. But it could also have been an undiagnosed disease, such as tuberculosis or cancer, complicated by a medically induced addiction to morphine acquired during attempts at treatment. We never know. Taking Henry's side, having a sick wife, let alone an addicted sick wife, if it was true, could not have been pleasant.

Henry Schoolcraft, it should be said here, was something of a cold fish. He was described as "lacking warmth" by one scholar and comes across in his writings as dull, pompous, and literal minded. One of his hobbies was collecting Indian skulls. He considered himself a student of craniology (an extant science), and at one point bragged that he had "two hundred eleven Indian skulls in my possession," which he was measuring with calipers. He could not ascertain why Indians, given that they were an inferior race, had larger heads. He concluded that it was the vigilance required of the savage's wilderness existence that created a bigger brain and surmised that "even the Greeks, in their pre-Hellenic period," probably had bigger heads.

He seemed to find Native Americans—as ultimately he was to find Jane—alternately fascinating and repulsive. On the one hand, he said he held his wife's Indian heritage in "the highest possible honor," and yet in his journals, he is unreservedly bigoted, describing the northern tribal groups as "untutored savages," who were universally "lazy" and characteristically "cunning and deceitful." Of the women, he says he "found little to admire, either in their collective morality or in their personal endowments."

The question has to be asked: what was Jane doing married to someone whose business it was to take lands away from her Native American relatives? And, conversely, what was Henry doing married to a woman who was a member of a race of people he may have found interesting but basically didn't respect?

They must have both been a little confused about their values, as people on frontiers in wartime are likely to be. They were not alone in forming an interracial marriage, but their marriage, as interracial marriages go, did not occur at a propitious time. As recently as 1802, Thomas Jefferson had publicly advocated such marriages, and the practice was widespread in any event. However, by 1830, once most of the lands had been acquired and Andrew Jackson's policy of removing indigenous peoples west of the Mississippi had come into play, the tide of public opinion against such marriages was turning.

The circumstances of Henry's life also changed during this same time frame. Up until the time Henry met Jane, he had been an explorer and ethnographer, and his views on indigenous people had been slightly more sentimental and romanticized. After becoming an Indian agent, when his work often put him in opposition to Indian interests, he became more negative and critical.

He had initially been opposed to the removal of indigenous people from their lands but was to change his mind and become an active supporter of such policies. He came to believe that, more than education or money, Christianity was the key to helping them. "All our attempts in the way of agriculture, schooling, and the mechanical arts are liable to miscarry," he wrote, "unless the Indian mind can be purified by gospel truth."

Henry Schoolcraft became more religious with the passing years, according to ethnohistorian Robert Bieder, author of *Science Encounters the Indian, 1820–1880: the Early Years of American Ethnology,* a book published by the University of Oklahoma Press in 1989. In a letter to Jane in 1830, quoted in Bieder's book, Henry exhorted Jane to make their household more devoutly Christian. He thought this would not be easy for Jane because of her background, "brought up in a remote place, without anything which deserves the name of a regular education: without the salutary influence of society to form your mind, without a mother, in many things to direct you, and with an overkind father."

Being a woman would increase the difficulty for Jane, Henry writes, because "it is the domestic conduct of a female that is most continually liable to error, both of judgement and of feeling. . . . Nothing is more clearly scriptural, than that a woman should forsake father and mother and cleave to her husband and look up to him with full confidence as, next to God, her guide philosopher and friend."

In 1833 Henry Schoolcraft relocated the Indian agency to Mackinac Island. This further isolated Jane from her family, to whom she was very close—especially her mother—and who had provided her with both economic and moral support.

Henry spent more time now traveling away from home. One suspects that there must have been a growing realization on his part, at least, and perhaps an apprehension on hers, that the changing times made his marriage to Jane—and the children it had produced—a drawback to his advancement in his career beyond the wilderness.

Jane Schoolcraft may have realized on Mackinac Island, if not before, that Henry was uninterested in spending time with her or their children. She might have contemplated the possibility that his work negotiating treaties, if successful, would result in the end of their union. She perhaps had known, at the infant William Henry's birth, that producing a child who looked Caucasian was her ticket to marital security and that the child's death would be her undoing.

On Mackinac Island we know that the Schoolcraft children attended the mission school in which Jane was active. "This excellent and accomplished, and intelligent lady," McKenney writes of Jane, "whose whole soul is in this work."

One of the few intimate glimpses we get of Jane Schoolcraft is from Anna Jameson, an Irish writer who journeyed with Jane from Mackinac to Sault Ste. Marie by canoe. She tells of a night, when the mosquitoes were out in swarms, and Jane stayed up all night, singing to her children and waving the mosquitoes away.

In 1836 Schoolcraft concluded the treaty with the Michigan tribes whereby they would cede most of the state. By 1838, Schoolcraft had taken the children, Janee, ten, and Johnston, nine, and placed them in eastern boarding schools.

In a poem written in Chippewa and translated into English, Jane writes of journeying away from her children through dark trees, a dark land, "I leave the bright land where my little ones dwell with a sober regret and a bitter farewell." By all accounts, Jane was a devoted mother who was heartbroken at being separated from her children.

The Schoolcrafts, by this time, were almost never together. On 9 May 1842, Henry left for England and on 28 May 1842, in the arms of her sister, Jane died.

Henry Schoolcraft returned to New York after his trip to Europe and for a time changed his name to Colcraft. He had been accused of misappropriation of government funds, and now "his failure to secure remunerative employment," biographer Richard Bremer writes, "contributed to the further deterioration of his financial condition." Robert Bieder characterized this time in Schoolcraft's life as "a time of debt and ravenous insecurity."

Beyond Henry's journals and letters and the few poems of Jane's that survive in the literary magazine that Henry published when they were first married, there are only a few secondary sources that shed light on the Schoolcraft marriage. One is a 697-page hyperbolic tome of Michigan chauvinism entitled, *Schoolcraft! Longfellow! Hiawatha!*, written by Chase and Stellanova Osborn. "To the Indians Henry Rowe Schoolcraft was a sun god," the Osborns note with no trace of facetiousness.

A more obscure book, written by Schoolcraft's second wife, Mary Howard Schoolcraft, is called *The Black Gauntlet*. This book, described by virtually everyone as memoirs or thinly disguised fiction—including the Osborns, who liked it—is a book about Henry's relationship with his first wife and their children.

Henry Schoolcraft met Mary Howard in 1846, and they were married in 1847. She was a spinster from a family of southern planters. Mary Howard owned "at least twenty" people as slaves, biographer Richard Bremer recounts, and adds, "This valuable asset no doubt enhanced her attraction to the Indian scholar."

In *The Black Gauntlet*, subtitled, *A Tale of Plantation Life in South Carolina,* southern belle Mary Howard Schoolcraft fictionalizes herself as Musidora Wyndham and Henry as Roland Walshingham. She dedicates the book to Henry Schoolcraft, whom she calls by the pet name, *Ne na Baim,* which she says is an Indian word meaning husband.

Part of this book is a proslavery tract. "Fie! Fie! on that abolitionist scourge," she writes. "It is a high moral vocation to civilize and christianize the heathen . . . to keep them in bondage until compulsory labor has tamed their beastliness."

The book is also a description of Henry's marriage to his "northern Pocahantas," which the author says took place in a burst of "ethnological enthusiasm." The children of this union saw their mother "as an angel of kindness" compared to Musidora, and they greeted "poor Musidora" with "freezing inhospitality." Relationships with Henry Schoolcraft's children were never good after this second marriage.

The Schoolcrafts adopted an eleven-year-old child who eventually married and gave birth, but both mother and child died soon after. There were no progeny of Henry Schoolcraft who survived. Johnston never married and, according to Mary Schoolcraft, fell prey to the weaknesses of his race. Janee became engaged to a man who lost his mind the week before they were to be married. She eventually married again, but never had children.

Henry Schoolcraft, as his biographers, the Osborns, put it in their inimitable style, "had his chain of new days on the earth come at last to its final links on December 10, 1864, in his seventy-second year, of dry mortification of the parts."

What is left of Jane and Henry's life together that is visible is Sault Ste. Marie. I visited there one warm day and sat on the edge of the canal and watched as one ship after another came down through the locks.

The locks dominate this town—and with their uniformed guards and fences along the canal—give it the feeling of an army post, duplicating in aura, if not in fact, what this town must have been like in its Fort Brady days when Henry built his Indian agency on the St. Marys River and negotiated treaties out of it.

I sat in the park near the canal and watched the waters of the St. Marys change color, in the way Anna Jameson described the waters of Lake Ontario changing color, like a dying fish, from gray to ruby to palest green, to silver and rose. Some students from Lake Superior State University came down to sun themselves by the canal, but they knew nothing of the Schoolcrafts and suggested I go up to the Soo Locks information center.

At the Locks there was no one on duty who knew about the Schoolcrafts. I ended up looking at photographs of the locks in various stages of construction: half-built, three-quarters built, all done. A lady outside on the steps, handing out brochures for tours of the locks, said she didn't know, but she thought Schoolcraft was one of the founders of the town.

Oryana

Several weeks ago I was in Traverse City's Oryana Food Co-op on Randolph Street making a small purchase of wild rice so I could stuff a turkey for a feast. I happened to be next in line after a small, nondescript, older man who was buying what looked like about half a pound of cracked black Java pepper, and I said to the clerk as I came through, "That man just bought pepper and that's all; isn't that interesting?" And she said, "Not only that, he does that about once a week."

I thought that was fascinating and decided one day when I had a few hours I might just come and camp out at Oryana and see what people bought all day. Oryana is an interesting place anyway, being sort of a cross between Zabar's (New York City's famous food emporium) and the kind of food co-op you might find in any college town. It combines financial success with sixties idealism, making it an anomaly certainly among food co-ops, and maybe in the business community.

The day I find to drive in from Lake Leelanau, the sky at 7:30 A.M. is pink and the waters of Grand Traverse Bay are blue. I feel like I'm driving in a dreamscape. I pass several joggers. I begin to daydream about Aspen, where I've never been, and San Francisco, where I've been a few times, and wonder if Traverse City is like these places, as I've heard it is. I think about places with beautiful landscapes and wonder if scenery alone inspires idealism. Or maybe it's something in the air. Or maybe this is nonsense.

I arrive at a square building at the corner of Maple and Randolph, facing the bay. The co-op used to be downtown on Front Street in a dusty upstairs loft with rickety stairs and an Indian-print bedspread for a doorway, but good management and the growth of the natural foods market have brought it to its new quarters. The building is functional but attractive with highly polished oak floors and hand-carved oak woodwork.

The only other person there at 8:30 in the morning is Brad Shugart and his giant dog, a Newfoundland, outside at the back door. Brad is a Leelanau County fruit farmer. He is mopping the floors. He says he is a longtime member and has been involved in the co-op for years.

The next to arrive are Debra Trowbridge and David Poinsett. Debra is a full-time co-op employee and is the one who agreed to my being there this morning. David is coming in to buy a few things. He is a self-employed designer of electrical circuits for meteorological equipment. Everyone is talking about the unseasonably warm weather. "Let's hope the jet stream stays up in Canada," David says. I must be the only one there who doesn't know what the jet stream is, because when I ask, everyone is able to explain it is a high band of wind circling the globe from west to east, like a belt, and when it shifts south from its usual place over Canada, it brings cold air with it.

John, or "Jack," Archiable comes in. He is a working member, which means, on this particular morning, he is going to dish up pasta primavera and package it in little plastic containers. The pasta primavera sells for $1.40 a pound and is redolent with fresh garlic.

The co-op officially unlocks the front door at 9 A.M. and the first customer is a blonde woman in a tweed derby and a yellow T-shirt. The T-shirt says, One World Music Tour 1984 on the back and Black Uhuru King Sunny Ade on the front, which she explains is a great reggae band and friends of hers. She buys two cups of Dr. Bronner's almond soap and two quarts of milk. She brings her own container for the soap.

At 9:15 a young mother with braces on her teeth and a baby in a cart comes in and buys egg rolls, tofu, whole wheat spaghetti, mozzarella cheese, and bread. She says she comes to the co-op because she wants to buy natural foods for her family. She says she is concerned about the pesticides and additives in food.

At 9:20 a businessman in an expensive suit comes in and buys a gallon of fresh-pressed apple cider. He says he is an insurance broker. He goes down the steps and across the tree-lined street and gets into an expensive-looking gray car. It is a very shiny car and the sunlight glints off the hood of it. Everything outside looks shiny, like things seen in a mirror. Everything has double outlines.

At 9:25 a woman who describes herself as "a mental health worker, a counselor, I guess a social worker," comes in and buys fresh-baked sprouted wheat bread, fresh primavera, soysage (a soy product that tastes like sausage), milk, several kinds of fruit, and what she calls "the most wonderful cookies in the world, fingerprint almond." She says she is on her way to Grand Rapids to a meeting and wants something "for the trip." She is white-blonde with an accent. "Latvia, have you ever heard of it?" she asks. "*Manny, manny* years ago." Then she is on her way in the sunny day.

At 9:35 a teacher comes in because, he says, "I'm hungry and it's my hour off and the teacher's credit union is right across the street."

At 9:40 a dark-haired woman in a hunter-brown corduroy jacket comes in and buys "David's lunch"—a piece of spinach lasagna, blueberry walnut cheesecake, corn and sesame snack, all-natural boysenberry juice, and something she calls "my staples"—millet tempeh, tofu, whole wheat flour, fresh spinach, gallons of different kinds of juice. "We eat a lot of tempeh and tofu because I'm into *quick* meals," she says, "and there's good protein. I do about one tempeh and one tofu meal a week." The co-op makes its own tempeh and tofu in a newly acquired kitchen across town.

I decide to visit there and find a small kitchen with an enormous black institutional stove and a little woman, so busy I don't ask her name, making tofu peanut butter pie with carob and rainbow salad with spiral pasta in shades of orange, ruby, pale wheat, and muted green, exactly the color of carrots, beets, pale wheat, and spinach.

Traverse City looks good in the morning sunlight as I drive back across town toward the bay and Randolph Street.

Back at the co-op a woman in a dress with balloons all over it says she comes all the way to the co-op from Bellaire because it's cheaper and has things she can't get anywhere else. She is a spritely older woman. She likes the idea of telling me what she bought. "These are things I can only get here," she says, as she puts Amaretto coffee, pastry flour, red winter wheat flour, six-inch pieces of ginger root, allspice, cinnamon stick, and cloves in a box. "Cheaper," she says, as she adds walnuts, yeast, and powdered milk to her order.

At 11:10 a young girl and an older man are at the checkout. The girl is very beautiful—she looks like a young Gibson girl—and the man is very distinguished looking. The girl is buying rose hip tea, peanuts, sunflower seeds, and vitamins. She is an art major at Interlochen Arts Academy and her father with her is visiting from Arizona. "I don't come here a lot, because I don't go anywhere a lot," she says, "but when I can I like to come here. It is like a favorite store of mine in San Francisco."

Ann Arbor Again

I am out of the northern hills along Lake Michigan and past the swamps of Mesick and into a gas station near Clare by 8 A.M. There is no dawn, just a thinning of the dark into an overcast winter morning. Up north, we pump our gas and then pay for it. Here, I pay for it first, then pump it. Standing there, I am aware of having crossed some invisible line into a land where the prospect of theft is part of the most everyday transactions.

The bruised purple and ruby landscape of late November floats by beyond the thruway. JFK memorials are on the radio. In Dallas they have built an assassination museum: Ted Kennedy is objecting to it as tasteless. I am on my way to Ann Arbor to see how much the campus has changed in the twenty-five years since I went to school there.

The University of Michigan in the 1960s was considered one of the most radical campuses in the United States. This was where the first teach-in against the war in Vietnam was held. This was where the radical underground was born, when a man accused of bombing the Ann Arbor CIA office disappeared into it.

In his book, *Cycles of American History,* Arthur Schlesinger, Jr., says this country goes through thirty-year cycles of social change, and that "shortly before or after the year 1990, there should come a sharp change in the national mood or direction," which will be revealed in a "renewed sense of public purpose."

If that is true, I am thinking as I drive past the slag piles along the Saginaw River, one should be able to pick up on that renewed sense of public purpose in that murky mirror of American cultural change, the college campus. My daughter, now a freshman at the university, has told me little seems to be happening there, but I want to see for myself.

The Ann Arbor campus in the blue November sunlight looks smaller, more threadbare than I'd remembered, yet at the same time so familiar that a wave of recognition passes through me like electric shock, threatening to glue me to the floor of the Nichols Arcade, near where I've gotten out of my car.

What I'm trying to do with this trip, I decide, is figure out the mood of the country so I can locate myself in relationship to it. I have sensed for months that this country is in for a cultural tectonic plate shift, and I've come to Ann Arbor because I think I will be able to feel it here, like a tremor in the ground. But the sheer enormity of this project hits me, and for a moment I lean against the window ledge of Van Boven's men's clothing store to think about it. What would Rip van Winkle have done, I ask, on finding himself in his old town after a twenty-five year absence? Rip, I decide, would stay calm and wander around and talk to people.

I've been given permission to attend the class of a professor I had talked to on the phone—William Alexander's seminar on American documentary film—and on the spur of the moment, for lack of a better plan, decide to go there. I make my way toward Angell Hall, a building that resembles the Parthenon, and then, because the vast granite steps seem to be undergoing repair, around to the other side, to Mason Hall and the Fish Bowl.

What's strange is I recognize the smell of Mason Hall. Scanning bulletin boards along the way, I see notices everywhere that relate to racism: the myth of the black male rapist; a series of university-sponsored workshops on racism; a protest of the university's new report on minority affairs.

The light on the third floor of Mason Hall is as dim as always, as if a fuse had blown, and the roofline of the buildings out the window on North University matches some neuropathic memory in my head, creating instant déjà vu. The students in this small classroom look no different than students in the late sixties. My generation introduced blue jeans as regular dress, and that, if nothing else, has stayed. As we wait, I ask them about the racism notices I've been seeing on bulletin boards. "It's a very paranoid atmosphere right now," says one square-jawed young man, "with everyone saying, 'You're a racist, you're a racist.'"

I ask what they should do about it. There's a long silence. What do you *feel* about it? I ask. "In some ways I feel all we can do is wait," says a young blonde woman in blue jeans. A bearded young man in an argyle sweater says, "I don't think the university is a good place to push these ideas forward. It's a good place to intellectualize these things."

There is one black student in the class, a young man with dreadlocks, casually but expensively dressed, who says, "I find it hard to believe blacks are going to do the morally correct thing. All the great leaders have been neutered—King, Malcolm—so what's going to happen when blacks try to achieve equality through passive resistance?"

When I leave I go through Angell Hall, vaguely looking for the wire service machine that used to be there where I first read the news of John F. Kennedy's assassination on 22 November 1963. I can still remember standing in the watery greenish light, feeling the numb disbelief of all of us standing there, and hearing the "click-click, click-click-click" of the teletype machine.

My room at the Michigan League across the street from the old, dark-brick Chemistry building is old-fashioned comfortable. Chenille bedspreads, windows that open. It has started to drizzle outside. Down the hall, two young white maids, nonstudents from Ypsilanti, are going from room to room, making beds and watching "The Young and the Restless."

In my day only women could stay at the Michigan League, and it was called the Women's League. Now both men and women stay there, and we all have that clubby, alumni look. Or as my daughter said later about the League, "Everyone in

there, even the young people, looks as if they were born before 1920."

Out the back door of the Michigan League, in a structure that looks like a ship, is the new University of Michigan Alumni Center. It is all glass and narrow stairs and steel-railinged balconies. Robert Forman, alumni director for twenty-three years, says the new president of the university, James Duderstadt, has pledged to make U of M a model of diversity in the twenty-first century.

"This is a new America," Forman says. "Our demographics tell us that pluralism isn't a thing of the future, it's here now." Or as his black assistant Richard Carter says, "The jury is in."

The demographics are startling. Taken from a report by Harold L. Hodgkinson called *All One System,* they say that by the year 2000, minority children will be one-half the U.S. school population and not to educate them will spell ruin for the U.S. economy.

The cafeteria of South Quad is noisy; clattering trays, milling students. I ask my daughter if it's my imagination or if black students and white students are eating separately. She says it's no optical illusion. Her friend Emily Li, from Hawaii, who's eating with us, says Asians are segregated, too, self-segregated, although less so than blacks. Emily finds the whole atmosphere so discomfiting she wants to transfer to the West Coast, closer to home. I don't remember segregation among students in the sixties; I think there were fewer minorities on campus then, and more openness.

I ask my daughter Lilah what she feels her social responsibility is, in terms of promoting equality. "A lot, Mom," she says, "but right now I feel it's all I can do to study for my calculus exam." She tells me I should talk to Kyra Keene, the roommate of a friend, who lately, in the last two weeks, has started listening to Malcolm X tapes.

Keene is tall, black, and stunningly good looking. I don't know what I'd expected from someone listening to Malcolm X tapes, but what I find in Kyra is someone who looks like she just stepped out of the Huxtable family on "The Cosby Show." She is from Shaker Heights, Ohio, where her father is a retired banker and her mother a librarian.

Racial incidents on campus began two years earlier, Keene says, with racist jokes on the campus radio and Ku Klux Klan-style fliers under the doors of black students. Her husky voice becomes huskier as she talks about it. More recently, Keene says, the student newspaper, the *Michigan Daily*, published composite drawings of a serial rapist showing the man to be black, about six feet tall, weighing 160 pounds, and between the ages of twenty and twenty-five.

"It could have been anyone," Keene says. "I've heard from my black male friends that they'd be walking down on campus late at night and they'd hear someone say behind them, 'Oh, my gosh, I think that's him.'"

South Quad looks more like a parking ramp than a dormitory, I think as I leave. Outside it is overcast. At three in the afternoon it looks as if the sun is already going down. Everywhere are students, walking, laughing; students like my daughter and Kyra Keene. I feel alternately like one of them and like everyone's mother as I wend my way toward what I think is the *Michigan Daily* on the other side of the Michigan Union.

I stop by the back door of the Union and ask an elderly woman in a beige coat who is holding dried baby's breath where the *Michigan Daily* is. She says, "Ah, yes, Arthur Miller knew it well," and directs me. It's then I notice the stains on her coat, the bright spots of rouge on her cheeks, the shopping bags filled with food scraps about her feet. The shock of this will stay with me for a long time. Later, when I tell my daughter Lilah about it, she will tell me homeless and impoverished people routinely scavenge for food scraps from the leftovers on students' tables in the Union dining room.

Playwright Arthur Miller had worked at the *Daily* in the thirties, I recall as I walk, when the big radical movement on campus had been communism. And in my day, Tom Hayden had been editor, before his national prominence as a leader of Students for a Democratic Society. The *Daily* had always had a reputation, as far as I knew, not only for radical, cutting-edge views but for excellence, and had several times bested the *Harvard Crimson,* both in coverage and awards. I was baffled by charges of racism leveled *at* the paper, instead of *by* the paper; it wasn't what you'd expect.

The *Michigan Daily* is in an old brick-and-ivy, Monticello-style building. "Racism is the issue that's rocked this university this year," says student editor Rebecca Blumenstein. "We printed composites of a serial rapist that showed the rapist to be black and were accused of perpetuating the myth of the black male rapist. We can only print the news. We can't change the news. The fact is, the rapist was black."

I spend hours walking around the town under a sky of slushy snow clouds thinking about this. Virtually every black student I talked to thought the composites were too generic to be useful, racially insulting and bad journalism. Almost every white student I spoke with either didn't know about the issue, didn't understand the issue, or agreed with Blumenstein.

I walk down to Neilsen's Greenhouse where my son Jesse's father used to work. He would bring me flowers—daisies, roses, ageratum, freesias, amaryllis—wearing those coveralls that made him look like Mr. Greenjeans on Captain Kangaroo. I walk around in the park along the Huron River among the tangled ropes of fog and rain, thinking about how I used to push Jesse in his stroller here.

I walk back up the hill and then down to the Farmers Market, near Braun Court, where I once lived—a courtyard of turn-of-the-century dairy workers' houses, now transformed into fancy restaurants. I walk to the Treasure Mart resale store. Then I walk back the way I had come. I get barbecued ribs from De-long's. It is snowing. The homeless are everywhere, young and old, black and white, male and female. They all look grayish and as if they have been whipped.

At dusk I turn and walk up Division Street, past St. Andrew's, where several of the homeless are gathered in the church narthex, up Lawrence Street, where I lived at Vail Co-op. Up State Street. In the distance I hear a train pass with a sound like a jazz saxophone.

Outside the Michigan Union the black branches of the wet trees are backlit by a mauve sky. I notice a convoy of Asian students in youthful and expensive cars, with some students getting out of some cars and into others and vice versa; musical cars. Perhaps they are on their way to a party.

Hispanic students are not much in evidence on the U of M campus, even though the Hispanic population nationwide is the fastest-growing minority and is expected to equal or exceed the black population by the year 2020. At the regents' meeting I'd attended the day I arrived, Anne Martinez, president of the

Socially Active Latino Students Association (SALSA), said there were only eighty-five Latino students on campus and of those, forty would drop out before graduation because of a hostile or indifferent educational atmosphere. The university has appointed fifteen new black faculty and several new black administrators in the last year, but Hispanics say they have not received the same treatment.

I see no Native American students on the Ann Arbor campus, although I am told there are thirty of them, up from fifteen the year before. In 1978 the university successfully fought through the courts to deny that the Fort Meigs treaty required the school to educate students from Michigan tribes free of charge in lieu of payment for their land.

My daughter Lilah has told me not to walk around alone at night, and so even though my feet seem to want to carry my mind around this town indefinitely, I return to the Michigan League, my walled city, in past the lone night attendant, who is sitting like a figure in a dream in a straight-back chair by the elevator, a pale, wispy blond man, knitting a red sweater.

Saturday morning the sparrows in the ivy of Hill Auditorium are twittering madly against the cold. Someone once told me half of them will die in a cold winter. The clock on Burton Tower says it's six; I can't look at it without thinking about the university regent Sarah Power who jumped from the tower in 1987.

The morning star hangs above the crook in the road on North University, just the way it always did. I make my way toward the "diag" and South University, thinking I might go sit in the Quaker Meeting House on Hill Street the way I used to as a student.

The basement of the Quaker Meeting House is where I worked in the Children's Community School. The directors of the school in 1968 were Bill Ayers and Diana Oughton, two students from prominent and wealthy Chicago families. Bill's father was president of Commonwealth Edison and Diana's father was a banker who'd headed Nixon's campaign. I can still remember Diana coming in one day crying because the woman she student-taught for in the public school had graded the children's valentines. The Children's Community School was an alternative school, and one of the things it was an alternative to was grading valentines.

The Ann Arbor campus in the sixties was considered a radical crossroads in the heart of the Midwest. Students were constantly coming and going—to lunch-counter sit-ins in the South, teach-ins against the war in New York, and marches for peace in Washington, D.C. The sense of high moral purpose and noblesse oblige was contagious, and when I graduated in August of 1968, I decided to stay and work for little or no money in the Children's Community School rather than take a regular teaching job in Boston.

I moved in with Bill and Diana that fall, only to be disappointed when the school folded for lack of funds. I did substitute teaching, and Bill and Diana became increasingly active in Students for a Democratic Society. That year, I realized later, was probably the turning point in their transition from fairly ordinary student radicals to people who would later found the Weathermen and the Weather Underground, violent political subgroups, largely disowned by others in SDS. But by December 1968 I had moved out and we lost touch. In March 1970 I read in the papers where Diana had accidentally blown herself up making bombs in a New York townhouse; she was identified by her little finger.

It was like learning that a member of your Brownie scout troop had become a mad bomber. There was tremendous idealism in the early sixties that gave way to tremendous frustration in the late sixties as the war dragged on and abridgment of civil rights increased. This produced a rigid, violent idealism, which, if you think about it, may be the course that every revolution runs.

We had the luxury of idealism in my day. Students in the sixties were more affluent, more naive, and more sheltered from the grim realities of everyday life. There was the war, but it was far away. Our graffiti were peace symbols and Make Love,

Not War. Now students on the Ann Arbor campus go to classes on sidewalks dotted with red, spray-painted female forms and the words "A Woman Was Raped Here" and cannot escape daily reminders of crack, AIDS, and the homeless. By comparison, we had an easier time of it.

Diana Oughton was a serious woman, steely of will, literal minded. In high school she'd worked as a maid for a black family because she didn't think it was fair that blacks should be maids for whites and not the other way around. In some ways it didn't surprise me to learn she had been making bombs to put in federal buildings as a way to stop the government from sending bombs to Vietnam. We had all seen the photos of the napalmed Vietnamese child running naked in charred pain. Diana wanted to put an end to that; instead, she put an end to herself.

The mood on campus this November 1988 weekend doesn't resemble anything I remember from my time as a student. Then the air was electric with the hopes of ending the war in Vietnam, improving civil rights. Now there is a mood of tension, frozen emotions from many white students and a sense of carefully considered protest from black students. The polarity between the two groups is disturbing.

One student in South Quad, when I had asked what could be done about racial injustice, had said, "What injustice?" These words play over and over again in my head as I walk back to the Michigan League. Denial is what I hear on the playback. Certainly this country was built, in part, by our nation's willingness to take from the Native Americans and enslave the Africans and then deny the harm done by it. I can't tell if students are simply overwhelmed by this world they have inherited and can't deal with it all, or if they feel they have privileges and material wealth *because* other people don't have them.

There is hardly anyone I know left from the sixties on the Ann Arbor campus. One person who is, is Robben Fleming. He was U of M president from 1968 to 1980 and was interim president in 1988, before James Duderstadt took over in October.

He has graciously agreed to see me on this gray Saturday morning, describing his house over the phone as "a white bungalow" off Washtenaw. November leaves are piled in the gutter and a cold rain is falling as he opens the door for me. His house and his style are unpretentious. Cream-colored carpets, cream-colored walls, like my grandparents' house, clean and homey, dishes in the sink, unraked backyard.

"The times are quite different now," he says. "Then, the draft created an uneasiness. Civil liberties were at a different stage—those were the days of the Bull Connors [the southern sheriff who turned dogs and fire hoses on demonstrators]. It's probably more civilized today; students are somewhat more conservative."

He is genial, avuncular, charming in that way of men of the old school. I can remember Bill Ayers saying how Fleming reminded him of his father.

Addressing current problems with racism on campus, he says, "I don't think there's any doubt that [racism] occurs, and that's a great tragedy—but I don't think anyone understands how complicated the problem is."

I ask why the university has only about two hundred and ninety incoming black freshmen, or five percent of the incoming students, when eight hundred would be needed to bring it to thirteen percent, which is the percentage of the state's black population.

"The key is *qualified* minorities," Fleming says. "You have to remember, the University of Michigan in its origin was really a private school. There wasn't even a state here in 1817." I must look startled and begin to say it's been a state school for over a century and a half, when he muses, "Blacks have suffered. I suppose since the days of slavery."

I ask why the university doesn't increase minority enrollment with Asian students, who I understand are qualified.

"But if you do that," Fleming says with a smile, "you get complaints not only from the black community but from the white community."

Monday morning dawns sunny and cold.

In a room of what used to be the engineering school, a young black woman named Barbara Ransby, a graduate student in history who did her undergraduate work at Columbia University, and a spokeswoman for the United Coalition Against Racism says, "A lot of the words Duderstadt is using now [about the need for minority enrollment] are words we have given him. I don't see anything in his history that shows this is a culmination of long-standing commitment. I don't want to psychoanalyze Duderstadt. I think he's a pragmatist."

Thumbtacked to the wall above her head is a striking poster with flaming gold letters saying, "Carrying the Torch," and then under that in smaller letters, "Women in the Civil Rights Movement 1941–1965," and it shows a long line of women, some of them pushing baby strollers, some of them carrying babies, some of them holding children by the hand, some of them young, some of them old, and some of them carrying flags, marching, and the words: "Trail Blazers and Torch Bearers."

Ransby says the reason the university has failed to significantly increase minority student enrollment is that their criteria are flawed. The standardized tests, for instance, are culturally biased, and there are other criteria that are missing. "We need to look at the whole person," she says. "We need to go to a personal interview. We need to look at the person who has Bs, but is working two jobs or doing community service."

A bright-eyed child plays near her as she talks. She introduces him as her son. I make reference to Martin Luther King's "I Have a Dream" speech and ask her where she thinks the dream is going. She is thoughtful for a moment, then she says, "Near the end of the civil rights movement, people were coming to the understanding of the interconnectedness of different struggles. So we're coming to the point that we are not only concerned simply with integrating the most oppressed sectors into the mainstream, but in creating a fundamentally more humane society."

An hour after speaking to Barbara Ransby I am in Charles
Moody's office—after paying two City of Ann Arbor parking
tickets that I've gotten that weekend. Moody is the newly appointed black vice provost for minority affairs, who readily
admits he was hired in the wake of student protest spearheaded
by the powerful United Coalition Against Racism. I blurt out
to him that when I applied to U of M from the state's tiny
Leelanau Peninsula, I knew my multiplication tables halfway
through six, had studied history under a woman who used to
tell us to outline a chapter while she read *True Confessions,* had
flunked everything my junior year out of spite and boredom,
and could scarcely have had a worse education or worse attitude
than the most disadvantaged minority kid, so why can't the
university find eight hundred black freshmen?

"You got in because you are *white,*" Moody fairly spits the
words at me. That and the fact that my father could pay and
three of my sisters had gone there, is my thought; and those
things were also true largely because I was white.

"We are a world nation," Moody, fifty-six, says. "By the
middle of the twenty-first century, white people will be 9 percent of the global population." Educating minorities is "an economic necessity," Moody says. "I'm not asking you to educate
minorities out of moral goodness, or fairness, or justice. It's
survival."

As I wait to see President Duderstadt, a floor down from
Moody, I think about the fortlike construction of this Fleming
Administration Building, with its small, bulletproof windows,
built in the wake of the violent sixties. "I guess people didn't
want to get shot at in their offices," one young student explained it to me, like an archaeologist reconstructing a dead
culture.

My mind drifts to a time when white people will be even less
than 9 percent of the population and there are shops along the
expressways that say Caucasian Arts like the ones that now say
Native American Arts. And when you stop at them there will

be people of color running the shop and they will tell you the Caucasians are "good with their hands." There will be little wooden napkin holders with hearts and ducks and maybe in one corner an old white woman knitting pink and blue baby booties and people will go up to her and say, "Are you a real Caucasian?" and people like me and General Westmoreland will populate the prisons, and sociologists will do studies about how violent and aggressive the Caucasian race is and develop programs to educate us, although everyone will know what a stubborn, stiff-necked, uneducable race we really are.

Duderstadt is a tall, fair-haired man who grew up in a small town in Missouri, did his undergraduate work at Yale, graduated summa cum laude, and began his career at U of M in the nuclear engineering department in 1969. He was appointed by Ronald Reagan to a five-year term on the National Science Board in 1985 and chairs that board's Subcommittee on Education and Human Resources. He was provost from 1986 to 1988 before becoming president. He is forty-six—my generation.

I ask why the university is moving so slowly on minority enrollment, which has increased only about a percentage point for black students in five years, going from 4.9 percent in 1983 to 6.2 percent in 1988, and only increasing about two percentage points in the last year for all minorities, in the total student body of 32,400, from 13.5 percent to 15.4 percent, according to figures from the Office of Academic Affairs.

"We're not doing enough, that's why," Duderstadt says. "We could do more. We have to do more. We're grappling with the most significant challenge to our nation. It's not just minorities; K-through-12 education is abysmal. It's not just schools, it's the disintegration of American families. Few people seem to realize that human resource development will be the dominant issue of the 1990s. I understand the need for more prisons, but if we cannibalize our resources for the future of our children, what a tragic future we will have."

I ask him how he got to this point in his thinking.

"I saw the writing on the wall," he says.

If I see Arthur Schlesinger's "renewed sense of public purpose" looming in anything I have seen or heard in Ann Arbor, I do not feel it is the same kind of public purpose there was in the sixties. Then the desire for social change was fueled by moral outrage and characterized by idealism. The social changes I see and feel now in Ann Arbor are coming from a more mature perspective, are motivated by economic necessity, and are characterized by pragmatism.

Several people have said that events in the sixties—the national affluence and war in Vietnam—were so unique that the radical fervor of that time could never be repeated. This makes some sense to me, but at the same time, the labor unions and Communism of the thirties—to some extent precipitated by the Depression and the Communist revolution in Russia—were unique historical events, too. It seems possible to me that a radical movement centered around the homeless and the growing number of children in poverty could take place yet. A global economy and the emergence of women as a political force in Third World countries could create far-reaching changes. A race war in South Africa, which many say is inevitable, would have immediate repercussions in this country.

As I drive past the trendy shops on State Street on my way out of town, past streets filled with jean-clad students with their bikes and backpacks, past Border's Book Shop, I feel a mingled sense of relief to be leaving and a nostalgia for staying.

I am several miles out of town when I decide to turn around and go back and drive past the house on Felch Street where I lived with Bill Ayers and Diana Oughton in the fall of 1968. It was a tiny house, small as a dollhouse, in a middle-class black neighborhood beyond Main Street.

I go in under the railroad pass, which I didn't remember, up a hill where the houses seem to have been painted by Edward Hopper. The dollhouse is gone. Where it stood is a vacant lot, already gathering shadows in the November afternoon.

Five o'clock, somewhere between Midland and Farwell, it is nearly dark and new snow is blowing across the road, like long, looping loose skeins of soft, white angora yarn. The fields are black-green, tinged with purple. The almost-full moon is rising.

Four years later, on 2 May 1992, I am returning to Ann Arbor, again, to attend my daughter Lilah's graduation. I never went to my own graduation—no one did in those days—and so this will be the first one I have ever attended. Lilah is graduating at the top of her class, having made Phi Beta Kappa, something else with which I have only the remotest acquaintance.

The day Gaia and I drive down it is hot, humid, insect-breeding weather. It is only a day or two after an all-white jury acquitted four white policemen in Los Angeles of brutally beating Rodney King. I've heard on the news that the rioting in Los Angeles has spread to San Francisco where my son lives, and to Seattle, where my sister lives.

I am wondering what kind of mood I'll encounter in Ann Arbor. I can remember the Watts riots in the summer of 1965 and the Detroit riots in the summer of 1967 and the ripple effect they had in the nation's consciousness as well as in the cities so that just beneath the surface, depending on your color, was either fear or rage. Detroit looked bombed afterward; and still does in many places.

We parents and family members mill around the stadium off Main Street watching our children through the high wire fence. The graduates are pretty much self-segregated by race—blacks in one group, whites in another, Asians in still another.

I learn that in the last four years, since 1988, the university has increased minority enrollment for black incoming freshmen by 64 students, from 290 to 354. There are five more Native Americans, 36 now instead of 31. The number of Asian students has increased from 407 to 535, and there are 44 more Hispanic students among the incoming freshmen, an increase from 171 to 215. Yes, minority enrollment has increased, but so has over-all freshman enrollment. I remember what Duderstadt said about reading the writing on the wall, and I wonder what wall? What writing?

If anything there are visibly more homeless in the streets of

Ann Arbor now, during 1992 May graduation, than at any time previously. In March 1990 when I had been visiting Ann Arbor, the homeless had converged on the Ann Arbor City Council, complaining that the city was building parking ramps where before there had been low-income housing.

"The homeless aren't just going to go away and die," a spokesman for the homeless, black attorney Larry Fox, told the council. "They are going to *try* to survive. That's the *human drive*. And the more *crushed* they are, the *more* they will be pushed to crime and violence." He said taxpayers would pay for the homeless one way or another, either with exorbitantly expensive prisons and police protection, or less expensive ongoing human services and public education.

Graduation itself is a series of staging errors. Thousands of parents sit from 11:30 to 2:30 in uncomfortable, backless bleachers while it threatens rain. Thousands of students come single file—endlessly, like mice through mouse holes—through two, widely spaced, narrow openings. We all mindlessly watch them, having nothing else to do. This takes up an hour and a half. Nothing else goes on meanwhile.

Almost the entire parent audience looks to be white and well-to-do. Later, after the graduates file in, there are speeches but no one can hear them. A lady in front of me from Grosse Pointe says, "For football games they have loudspeakers." Who planned this graduation, is the question in my mind, and did *they* graduate? Maybe Lilah should ask for her money back.

But no matter, or rather, never mind. Lilah is pleased to be done with school. She still looks little and young. She has a bright future. On the way out of town Gaia and I go down South University. A store is selling Rodney King T-shirts that say, "No Justice, No Peace."

Farther on, down on Main Street, on our way north out of town—perhaps, I am thinking, seeing Ann Arbor for the last time for many years—there is a tent city set up on the front lawn of the city-county building. White children and black children, all poor, play in the dirt around the tents. Here there is no segregation. A sign on a tent wall says, Vacancy.

SNOW
DRAGONS

Winter

Winter is our season up north. It claims us. We have to claim it. Like an undertow, if you fight it, it'll wear you out. "Just submit," a friend said one winter. And I did. And it worked.

You have to love it. As you would anything difficult, dark, spare, strange. To embrace its oddness.

Winter is an exotic season, a season of surreal sensations, almost a subconscious season. Winter is the inward journey, the time of year when you learn, as Theodore Roethke said, " . . . not to fear infinity / the far field, the windy cliffs of forever, / the dying of time in the white light of tomorrow."

Winter begins for me with deer season—with sleet—with rain and snow mixed and that cold, wet wind down out of Manitoba, Alberta, Ontario—down from Moose Jaw, the Pukasaw, Thunder Bay.

We feel winter here, before it comes, with those shifts in wind coming across the lake. We can feel it even in June, but as soon as school starts in September, we can actually smell it on the wind. By the time the big lake storms come in October and November, we are feeling it daily.

From my kitchen window I can see the pines on the old railroad grade sway in the wind, sigh and sough in the wind, a wall of pines. The wind harp widens.

There are days in November when there is no light at all—when the cars have their lights on at noon, the whole day flat, dark, and glassy.

Days when one retreats to the warmth of the wood stove, to a heaven of house plants, red geraniums, English ivy, a day of fat, warm cinnamon buns fresh from the oven just as the school bus comes at 3:30.

At dusk red hunters disappear into the dark woods.

In December, red Christmas cacti bloom profusely all around the living room. Novena candles send out their diffuse light— devotional invitations. December first, the Advent calendar on the refrigerator. Each day my daughter Gaia, now twelve, but still loving this childish ritual, opens another window onto another world.

On a Saturday before the snow gets deep, we go back into the swamp behind our house to cut a Christmas tree. Red twig dogwood against a gray sky.

Beside the path, a beautiful, plump partridge flutters loudly through the highbush cranberries, startling me, so my heart itself seems to make the partridge's sound.

January blizzards, the driveway plowed six times in two weeks. White snow, purple shadows; the day the color of a turnip.

One day the January sun comes out, raw and bright. Ten below. I pile on layers of clothing: winter underwear, snowpants, two sweaters, a down jacket, extra socks, Sorrels; and go out into it. I walk the woods trail, solid from the trek of snowmobilers. Here the hills are quiet, peacefully sleeping, even at midday, and there is only the squeak of my steps in the cornstarch snow.

The sun is blinding, even here in the path between the hills. The trees creak and sway, as if they might snap in the cold. Their upper bodies contain no sap; it is all in their roots. Glancing up between the black trees, like piano keys, I see a trail on the snow-covered hill—no wider than a broom handle; almost invisible—winding down through the deep snow. At first I think it must be a small snowball, a clump of snow that fell from a branch and then rolled to the bottom of the hill. The trail is startlingly sinuous.

I follow it to where it would have come out on the snowmo-

bile trail. Here in the path are the faintest signs of struggle, a little blood, a few gray, downy feathers. A snake? No, a snake-like weasel, the thickness of a broom, wrestled a bird to its death, and then engorged it, beak and claws and feathers and all, and then slithered back under the deep snowdrifts toward the creek to digest its prey in some warm, underground winter den.

Along by the creek, I see skunk cabbage all but hidden beneath the drifts, their leaves are already producing enough heat to melt the snow in small, indented circles above them. I jump the creek and head up the hill above the marsh. I jump fast, pretending I'm a deer, zigzagging, pretending I'm a snake snaking. I run until I'm hot and out of breath.

The scent of my sweat, wafting up through the endless layers and coming out at the neck of my turtleneck, smells like roast beef. My sweat in summer smells like seaweed. Below me, on the other side of the hill, is a low-lying area that is crimson with the red twig dogwood. This acre or two of deep red above the white snow fills me with longing for spring.

We have a January thaw, then two weeks of blizzards. Gaia gets sick and stays home from school Tuesday and Wednesday. Thursday and Friday the school is closed because of "blowing and drifting" snow. Then I am sick. Then the hot water heater breaks. I lie in bed late at night, feverish, listening to the mice in the walls. I can hear them running, talking to each other. They are so energetic and I am so weak. One friend who visited, already on edge, was made more nervous by the mice. He said he pictured them breaking through the wall at some point, with little miner's lights on their heads, saying "We've reached the bedroom, boys." As I lie there sick, listening to them, I think they sound too big to be mice. Maybe they're chipmunks. They sound like they're the size of kangaroos.

My body feels like it's getting bigger, then smaller. This happened all the time when I was a child, this sensation of shrinking and expanding. My mind dreams, hallucinates. I am the bird filled with eggs that the snakelike weasel has wrestled to its death. Then I am the snakeweasel with monkey whiskers, curled around its life's energy source, sleeping until spring. I am high on the hills, a bearded and horned snake-dragon, then I am a small girl being chased by the dragon. At the last possible moment, just before it devours me, I turn and throw a stick, like a spear, into the dragon's open mouth, nailing him to the frozen snow where his inflated body now collapses like those Chinese paper dragons lying in the streets of Manhattan after New Year's.

I am sick with the flu for days; then a check I'd expected doesn't come. It's hard to fight entropy when you're sick and have no money and the hot water heater is broken. One afternoon, I fly into action and make vegetarian goulash. Gaia declines to eat it. I say to her, "I am an ailing, aging, indigent, single mother and you must eat this goulash because it is all we have."

She says, "Did you have to fold your hands when you said that?" We laugh and suddenly the back of winter is broken. A few days later the check comes and we get the hot water heater fixed, but it doesn't loom as all-important now, the way it had a few days earlier. We're moving away from the dead center of winter now and as we do, I almost miss it.

Then February, three weeks of subzero temperatures. We here in the north know how winter can split rocks and split psyches, too. These are the months when women fall in love with woodcutters and those helpful men with bright new yellow battery cables.

Late winter, clear nights, deep snow. The country towns at night under a canopy of stars. On full moon nights the snowmobiles race over the hard crust snow, their motors revving with a sound like sex, or the desire for it.

March thaw. One day the temperature rises to thirty or more and I go for a walk. Snow falls. Soft as clouds, soft as cloud horses. I move through them as if I am riding a cloud horse, or as if I am a cloud horse, finding the road by the snow banks. Any day now a hot chinook, a fierce and maverick forty-mile-an-hour wind, will take down six feet of snow in three days, but for now I am in a dreamscape, meditating, merging with snow, feeling how it feels to submit to another reality.

Northern Lights

The first time I saw the northern lights, I thought, "That's it?" All I saw was a faint brightness on the northern horizon, not much greater than that of the Milky Way and not much more interesting.

I'd been expecting something that resembled the pictures in my second grade geography book that showed a fan-shaped rainbow that looked as if it had been cut with pinking shears, with spears of bright pink, bright green, bright red, and bright yellow. Now *there* was something worthy of the name *aurora borealis*.

Several times after that, usually at beach parties when I was a teenager, I saw the northern lights again. Even then, when I was slightly older, under more romantic circumstances and with a greater willingness to romanticize life, not to mention the added enhancement of illicit alcohol, the lights never seemed like a big deal.

Someone explained to me that this far south—in the area of the Leelanau Peninsula and the forty-fifth parallel—the northern lights weren't as bright or colorful as they were thirty-two hundred miles farther north, at the North Pole.

Still later, living in Ann Arbor and Manhattan, I began to appreciate being able to see anything at all in the night sky and when I returned home to the Leelanau Peninsula had a renewed appreciation for the rarity of the northern lights, for the subtlety of their movements. I even imagined I could distinguish some fine shadings of pink and green in the softly moving lights I would occasionally see when driving home from late nights somewhere. The lights were gentle, almost imperceptible, as if friends were signaling each other with flashlights from opposite hills.

But this appreciation was not an appreciation of an observed and remarkable phenomenon so much as a kind of modern angst, that sense of contrast between the country night sky and the city night sky, a barely conscious but fairly harmless sentimentality about Nature—with a capital N—and what I perceived to be the simple things of life.

It wasn't until one night recently that I truly saw the northern lights in all their splendor for the first, and perhaps the last, time in my life, for I understand from talking to many people who have lived here over eighty years and who have also never seen anything like it that such a display occurs once in a lifetime at most.

Someone described it as "the sky on fire," another described it as "God." It was like a vision, or it inspired visions. It left people speechless, overawed, excited. Several people said they could not get back to sleep after witnessing the sky, and stayed awake all night writing, talking, calling their friends.

I was alone that weekend. My daughter Gaia was off visiting, and I felt the absence of her sunny presence in the house. I distracted myself by keeping busier than usual. After writing all day Friday and into the early evening, I decided to scrub the floors and scour the stove. I fell into bed exhausted at nine o'clock, and read myself to sleep with *Newsweek, Harper's,* the *New York Review of Books,* and a stack of *New York Times* from the preceding week or so.

The news of the world seems like flickerings on a distant screen here, and so it makes little difference if we tune into it when it's happening or a week later. I generally feel I've gotten my exercise after my weekly wade through the *Times.* I feel rather good about it and dutiful for "checking in." It was in this mood of accomplishment and connectedness to the larger world that I dozed off finally over the papers.

Around midnight, after I had been asleep for an hour or so, I heard a knock at the back door. This was the door on the woods side of the house, away from the road. No one ever comes down this back trail at night. This unprecedented exception gave my new German shepherd, Crusher, an opportunity to bark her head off.

Outside was my neighbor, Susan Och, dressed in her navy pea coat and red boots. Susan often has a look about her—a look that says, "Let us be up and doing, then, with a heart for any fate," and she had that look now. She had her golden lab puppy, Sammy, on a leash, and her body was thrown forward to balance the weight of her small, four-year-old daughter, Shelagh, whom she was carrying piggyback.

"Come out!" she said. "The northern lights are brighter than I've ever seen them." Sleepily I threw on a down coat over my nightgown and slipped my bare feet into a pair of Sorrels and went out into the snowy night with her.

I walked out into light so bright it made it feel almost warm outside. We could see our shadows in it. The snow was about a foot deep and still clean from the fresh snowfall earlier in the week, and the air smelled like cucumbers.

Above the snow, taking up half the sky, were moving lights in shades of rose petal pink and tropical fuchsia, sea mist green and Howard Johnson blue, champagne gold and new corn yellow. They were like the neon chiffon scarves of invisible dancers arcing across the night sky, and we moved under them, mimicking their movements with our own, as if the lights were choreographing us. We moved sleepily, staring up, losing our footing sometimes in the deep snow, laughing.

The colors seemed to be the very air we breathed; large-scale color therapy—breathable color.

I felt I was swimming in light, that I had swallowed the sky. The sky had me.

There was a depth to these lights in the sky above me that made me feel the scope of the universe, the presence of the infinite.

Susan knows all sorts of odd things, so I asked her if she knew how the northern lights work. She said the earth's atmosphere has gases in it, and that they give off light when they become "excited." Sunspots or solar flares send out waves of energy on a solar wind, and this gets funneled toward the earth's magnetic field. The energy waves knock electrons away from atoms in the air, and upon recombination the process causes the discharge of light.

I was a little dizzy by now, but Susan likes science, and even though her father said her college education was wasted on her, she enjoys having the knowledge she gained there, such as an understanding of how the northern lights work. And so she continued to elaborate, going on to explain how the northern lights are like a fluorescent light bulb.

It was all very abstruse to me—it didn't help that she kept saying how simple it was all the while she was explaining it— and I couldn't seem to get the gist of it. I felt like the dull-witted robber in the movie *A Fish Called Wanda:* no matter what the plan is, he can't keep the sequence straight and continually interrupts to ask, "What was the middle thing again?" It might have helped if I'd known how a fluorescent light bulb worked in the first place.

She said the earth's magnetic field pulls in atomic particles from a solar wind and the molecules collide and create the "light show" called the aurora borealis. I see *curtains* of light, *quills* of light, *spars* of light—luminous sky *lakes* of light.

Everything is made of atoms, Susan said.

We could *all* be light, if we could move fast enough.

The human body, too, is magnetically polarized like the body of the earth.

The ancient Egyptians referred to the earth with a hieroglyph that reads, *Ta Mari,* which translated means, "the earth is the magnet of the sky," or "earth, attractor of celestial energy."

Sometimes the aurora seemed to create a dome over us, a planet-sized, overturned bowl of soft light. Other times there were leaping spears of light that seemed to want to pin us to the ground with the sheer brilliance of their dazzling color and cosmic energy.

After a while Susan's little girl grew restless and we realized we were getting cold. So we said good night, and Susan walked back down the woods road and I slipped back into my warm house.

But I couldn't get back to sleep. Instead, I gave myself over to night thoughts, the way you do after you've been awakened at midnight and had your consciousness stirred to deeper levels.

I thought about the homeless—the *New York Times* seems to always be filled with endless articles about the homeless—wondering if any of them, wherever they might have been that night, had seen the northern lights—and went from there to Thomas Jefferson and democracy and Lincoln. It occurred to me that a free society requires the abolition of poverty just as it required the abolition of slavery. I lay awake for hours, planning ways to make the world better; something about the northern lights made me want to correct every street corner and bring it up to the level of their cosmic loveliness.

The next day I found Aristotle's *Meteorologica* in the library. In 350 B.C. he wrote that men perceived the aurora borealis or northern dawn as "in some way divine." He went on to say that the aurora can take the form of "chasms" or "trenches" in the night sky and are sometimes called by people "torches" or "goats." He didn't explain why people call the lights goats, but I thought it might be because of the bucking and rearing of goats, motions the lights seem to imitate.

The lights were not something one could digest alone, and I spent much of the next week finding people who also had seen them and asking them how they had felt when they saw them, what they had done afterwards. One man, Mike Chamberlain, said he had landed the biggest fish of his life during a night of northern lights. Ananda Bricker, an artist in Glen Arbor, said she had gone out and lain down in her yard and looked up at the lights and felt she was being bathed in light.

My friends Toni and Mark Stanfield and their sons Karl and

Eric watched the lights from their front deck overlooking Chandler Lake. They had moved up from downstate and had never seen anything like it in their lives. Their neighbor, fourteen-year-old Teya Smith, saw the display from nearly the same perspective, and it was she who put into words what everyone seemed to have felt that night. "The lights," Teya said, "made it seem that *everything* was possible."

Big Rock Resort

We live about sixty miles from the Big Rock Nuclear Power Plant, as the crow flies, across a couple bays of Lake Michigan to Charlevoix. Every once in a while—when there's something in the paper about Three Mile Island or some other nuclear power plant—someone will say, "If that plant at Big Rock ever goes, we're goners."

Like the people of *Brigadoon,* we live in fairly pristine isolation here on the Leelanau Peninsula. Our fears are not the daily ones faced by many urbanites, who must lock their homes and concern themselves with weapons checks in the public schools their children attend. Our fears are fears of "the real world," in some form, coming into our lives. Big Rock, with all its vaguely understood potential dangers, is the closest thing to that world.

Not knowing where the Big Rock plant was, I asked my friend Laurie Davis, who had attended public hearings in Petoskey on what the plant should do with its spent fuel rods. She tells me it's on Lake Michigan between Charlevoix and Petoskey, right off U.S. 31. "You can't miss it," she says. "Every time I drive by it, I cross my fingers."

I am ready for a good dose of reality by the time I finally visit Big Rock. The weather obliges with a dank, cold rain. Resort towns out of season—Atwood, Torch Lake, Charlevoix—roll by in the gloom.

The Big Rock sign says, "The Big Rock Nuclear Power Plant—a Good Friend and Neighbor since 1962." The sign resembles those used in national parks. "The Chippewa Indians called it 'Kitchiossining'—The Big Rock—and it remains an important landmark today. Once an area where tribes from all over northern Michigan gathered for spring and fall meetings, today it is the site of one of Michigan's most valued assets: The Big Rock Nuclear Power Plant." The sign strikes me as slightly off, like GM putting up a sign saying their new factory is on the site of historic Poletown, from which the residents were torn amidst much weeping and gnashing of teeth, but where they used to celebrate many a Polish holiday.

The road is narrow and winding, flanked by dark spruce. At the end of it is the power plant. It seems small and, in the rain, unprepossessing.

Charlie MacInnis, the PR man I'd talked to on the phone, is there to meet me. He seems upbeat, professional, educated. He is casually dressed. "Have you read *The Hobbit*?" he asks me as we walk down the little path through the woods to the public affairs building. "Because I call this area Mirkwood. I bring my little boy out here to find wood elves. I love to show the place off. It's kind of pretty around here."

"Where's the Big Rock?" I ask him.

He shows me a rock in the lake that looks like a large boulder. It is a remarkably undistinguished-looking rock.

Charlie MacInnis is a likable guy. He tells me he has two children, a boy and a girl. His wife is a nurse and works the night shift at the hospital in Petoskey. He says he was in journalism downstate but got fed up with the negative emphasis in the news, and decided to go into public relations. He tells me his wife had a cardiac arrest patient in the emergency room the night before. I learn his father was a coal miner.

"You talk about accidents," he says, "everyday dangers. Men getting crushed by coal cars. Black lung disease. We have had no fatalities associated with our nuclear power plants."

"What about exposure to radiation?" I ask.

"You get the breakdown of some ions," he says. "But the point is nobody knows for sure what low-level radiation does to people."

We go into an amphitheater with soft lighting and watch a slide show about how a nuclear reactor works. Then there's a show-and-tell about all the things that produce radiation in our everyday environment: radios, TVs, Coleman lantern mantles, even orange Fiestaware. "It's the uranium that makes that plate orange," Charlie tells me.

I excuse myself to use the ladies' room. There is a metal, stand-up shower in the ladies' room.

I return to Charlie and he outfits me for the tour: hard hat, safety glasses, and a dosimeter to measure whatever amount of radiation I might get—all standard gear that is required by the labyrinth of federal regulations covering nuclear power plants. We move outside and toward the foggy bay and the main building. "You can usually see fishing boats out there," Charlie says. "Fishing's great off the reactor because the water's so warm. The fish love it."

"Why is the water warm?"

"Lake Michigan water is drawn into the power plant to cool the turbines and then discharged back into the lake—unchanged."

I try to look at him, but he is looking out at the bay and rubbing his forehead, where there is a red patch of irritated skin about the size of a quarter.

"What about sabotage of the plant?" I ask him. "What if the Russians bombed it? What about simple human error? What about something you haven't thought of yet? What about the long-term damage from radiation in the soil?"

"That's not a concern. You're dealing with people's fears. People are afraid when they fly that the plane's going to crash, but that doesn't mean the plane's going to crash."

"But sometimes planes do crash."

"We have safeguards," he says, "all top secret. We have a security force larger than those of most small towns." He shows me the trailer of the federal inspector. "He can't even socialize with us. So there's no way he can be influenced to look the other way."

We are inside the building now, going through a safety check. My ID is checked, then I'm frisked. At every doorway I have to "pass," like when we were kids and used to play Secret Fort.

We are on the second floor. We pass a whole flock of engineers and workers. Everyone looks like the kind of people you see in ads for the Peace Corps. One large man with a beard comes out of an elaborately locked room and begins going over and over his beard with a dosimeter. Presumably, he is not concerned about possible exposure to Fiestaware.

We visit the laundry room where they wash the radiation out of everything. Charlie talks to people. I skim the brochures he gave me. One called *Nuclear Waste: Toward a Solution* says, "Prompt action is crucial, since power plants have only limited space in which to store the thirty tons of spent fuel rods discharged each year from a typical reactor. Nearly sixty thousand tons of this material will have accumulated by the end of the century."

Charlie is traipsing up a flight of noisy, metal grating stairs in front of me. "What about the nuclear waste?" I ask him. "Isn't this stuff the most toxic substance known to man? Isn't it toxic for twenty-three thousand years?"

"That's why we had the hearings a few years ago," Charlie says. "They didn't want us to ship it, so we had to store it here. The hearings were so we could expand our on-site storage." He shows me racks, like pool cue racks, buried underwater, where the spent fuel rods are stored. The light everywhere is murky green, as if we're underwater too. There is something too upbeat about this tour. Though I am drowning in information, I can't seem to find the bedrock of reality I was looking for, the answer to the question of ultimate danger.

"You're lucky we're shut down today," Charlie says. "Just a routine safety check of our equipment. This means you can go inside the containment sphere." We step through jaillike doors, which are locked behind us, and then into something that looks like a giant clothes dryer before I say, "I don't think I want to do this."

We go back outside. We are done. It is noon. The bleak gray rain coming down is almost comforting.

In the dark November of 1992, when we had more cloud cover than any November in recorded history, I decide to go back to Big Rock. I know it is due to shut down at the turn of the century and wonder if, since Chernobyl, people in the nuclear industry have a more sober view of nuclear power.

One of the pioneers of nuclear power, Glenn Seaborg, was born in Ishpeming, in Michigan's Upper Peninsula. Seaborg, who received the Nobel Prize in 1951 for his work in chemistry, thought that the nonmilitary uses of nuclear power would transform civilization and bring it to new heights. Many people thought that in the 1960s.

It is a day of traveler's advisories but it is the only day I can go. Gaia is with me; she is home from school because of teacher in-service.

Snow squalls come rhythmically off the lake. There will be a wall of blinding snow, then it will be suddenly clear and the sun will shine through like Bible pictures. It is a few years after Chernobyl, a couple of years after a raccoon short-circuited the Fermi 2 plant in Monroe, Michigan, and only a few months after Big Rock itself has been shut down by its own "automatic protective mechanism."

Tim Petrosky has replaced Charlie MacInnis, who has been promoted to the head office. He is not as genial as Charlie was. He doesn't offer to take my coat. After I've stood in his office several minutes, he offers me a chair stacked high with heavy manuals. "You can move those," he says, pointing his chin at the chair.

Big Rock is due to be shut down 31 May 2000, he says. It is the oldest operating nuclear power plant in the United States. Petrosky tells me the site will either be used for another power plant or returned to its natural state. I mention to him that I saw in the news where the plant was shut down for an emergency safety check a few months ago and ask him when that was.

"All right, " he snaps at me, "I can see where this is going."

I ask him what he means. "I can see how you're going to write your article," he says. He sees me writing this down, and then seems to change course. He tells me, with a weary sigh, like a teacher repeating a lesson to someone who is not very bright, "The nuclear industry is inherently safe because of all the safety checks."

I ask him again the date the plant shut down. "I don't know," he says unpleasantly. "Ask me something else." I try to establish eye contact but when I look at him, he looks out the window, or rummages in his desk. We proceed to talk in this fashion for about forty-five minutes.

I ask him about the cost of shutting down the plant and the cost of storing the nuclear waste. He says Consumer's Power has billed its customers in an ongoing way for these costs.

I ask him where the spent fuel rods will be stored. He tells me the federal government has planned to build a storage facility at Yucca Mountain, Nevada. "It will store it for ten thousand years."

I ask him when it will be finished. He says construction hasn't begun yet. I ask him why. He tells me the people of Nevada have not yet approved it. I ask him why they haven't approved it.

"The nuclear industry has not done a real good job of communicating the massive benefits of nuclear power," Petrosky says sourly. "There's a fear of the unknown and nuclear power is so highly technical."

From Petrosky's office I walk up a wooden ramp to the office of the federal nuclear safety inspector, Elden Plettner. He is a big, lantern-jawed man who tells me he is a veteran of Vietnam and worked on a nuclear-powered navy submarine during the war. He has calendar pictures of deer and flowers all around his office and a photograph of his wife and children on his bookcase. He is from Nebraska.

I know little about nuclear submarines. I ask him what happens if one blows up, do they leak radiation into the water? To my surprise, he blushes. Yes, he says. Then he corrects himself.

"There are two-foot-thick stainless steel containment walls." He uses his hands to show me how much two feet is. "It would be very difficult for them to leak."

"If one blows, the men die?" I ask. He nods. "The fish die?" I ask. He nods. "But they don't count?" I ask. He looks confused. "The radiation goes into the water?" He nods.

"It's like a mobile Chernobyl?" He doesn't answer, so I say again, "It's like a mobile Chernobyl?"

This time he nods but doesn't speak; after a moment he says, "The Hanford [Federal Nuclear] Reservation had some problems where there was a tank that unfortunately had a leak and unfortunately leaked into the groundwater." I am somewhat dumbfounded by his telling me this and am aware that my mouth is hanging open, gathering drool; as gracefully as I can I close it and swallow. My mind is making rapid calculations: if he's telling me this, it must be a big problem that he thinks I know about, or there are even bigger problems he's not divulging.

"These things happen," he says, in the manner of someone relaying information learned by rote, "because people are uneducated about nuclear wastes."

I ask him what will happen if the year 2000 arrives and Yucca Mountain still doesn't have the nuclear waste storage facility built.

He colors up a little. "Then they will have to make provisions to keep it here on site."

I know I should ask him if that's possible. I know I should ask him if it won't be unsafe or prohibitively expensive. I know I should ask him what will happen if no community anywhere will allow a nuclear waste disposal site to be built where they are, but I can't pursue this. It's like interviewing the captain of the Titanic as it's sinking. I feel I am shaming him by asking these questions, and shaming myself.

"This is all so complicated," I say. "Do you have any written information you can give me?"

He photocopies several sheets of statistics and then, as if thinking of just the very thing, he pulls two gargantuan books—each twice the size of a New York City phone book—off the shelf. They are from the National Cancer Institute, still in their shrink-wrap. I see they are on radiation-caused cancer.

"Are you sure you want to part with these?"

"You can bring them back if you're ever back this way."

I thank him and he sees my daughter and me out through a maze of hallways and doors.

Gaia and I are in the car and on our way out the Big Rock road, when it begins to snow again. The sun is shining, then it isn't. We make it as far as the roadside park just beyond the entrance and stop and let the dog out. We can see the Big Rock plant from here.

Back on U.S. 31, it continues to sleet and now at four o'clock it is already getting dark.

The car smells like wet dog. The two big books of statistics Elden Plettner loaned me are on the seat beside the dog. They are the color of Nyquil. Cars have their lights on. Lake Michigan is a strange shade of black.

"Look," Gaia says. She points to a place over the lake.

"I can't look, honey, I'm driving." Then I look.

All I see are rolling dark clouds. Then I see a hole in the sky, a circle where the clouds have parted and the bright blue of the sky shows through, like a summer day up there behind those clouds. All around this blue hole in the gray clouds—through the thin, crepe suzettelike borders of the encircling clouds—the sun is shining, like light through lace.

From Car Parts to Karma

The question is, what do people want? I am speaking here of "wanting" in the cosmic sense, an area where I've always been curious about what other people wanted. So with this in mind one Saturday, I got a couple friends to come with me halfway across the state to the Song of the Morning Ranch—a Yoga Retreat of Excellence, on the Pigeon River near Vanderbilt.

Also called Golden Lotus, the camp was established in 1970 by J. Oliver Black, a former auto parts magnate who amassed a thirty-million-dollar fortune in Detroit before being introduced to yoga by Paramahansa Yogananda, a man who visited America from India in the 1950s.

Yogananda is perhaps best known for his book, *Autobiography of a Yogi,* which I had been reading for a week, finding things such as "The intuition of astral beings pierces through the veil and observes human activities on earth, but man cannot view the astral world unless his sixth sense is somewhat developed."

Black, now ninety-three and referred to in the *Golden Lotus News* as "the Master's oldest living disciple," interested me because I wondered how he had made the quantum leap from manufacturing auto parts to dispensing yogic wisdom. I knew that in the 1960s he had taught yoga at the Detroit Institute of Arts and that he still went down to Detroit twice a year to teach Kriya yoga, described in the retreat's newsletter as "the quick 'airplane' method to God." Black did not give interviews, I was

told when I called the Song of the Morning Ranch, but if we wanted to pay five dollars a person, our group could eat dinner at the camp on Saturday and that evening take part in a yoga meditation, after which Yogacharya Oliver would answer written questions.

As we drove along the swamps and bottomlands between East Jordan and Elmira, I thought not about Black, but about my Pilgrim ancestors, about the hordes of evangelists on TV, and about America's cyclic, historic, almost frantic search for religious meaning and religious roots.

I was jolted by the auto's sudden rise up onto I-75 and then down again into Vanderbilt, a town that on this day seemed treeless and drained of all color. The aluminum propane tanks gleaming in the bright sun conjured up lives where one would be eager to see an astral being, but the lady at the party store said she had never been out to Golden Lotus, "although I understand it's nice," she added politely.

A short way out of town, the landscape became pleasantly rolling and the swampy woods hugging the road looked dark, womblike and inviting: a place for deer to winter-over. It was about four-thirty when we came to the Golden Lotus camp. We crossed a dam and on one side was a wide brown expanse of backed-up river water and on the other, down in the woods, were small, gold-domed buildings.

I recognized Black as he made his way to the dining room. He was older and more frail than his photographs indicated, but well preserved, wearing black dress pants and a dark sweater with a white carnation in the buttonhole, his white hair worn slightly long; he resembled the English mathematician, Bertrand Russell.

Although we arrived in the dining room within moments of when the gong sounded, everyone was waiting for us. Black was seated at the head of the table in an ornate high-backed chair that somewhat dwarfed him. The rest of us were seated on narrow, backless benches along either side of the long, narrow table.

The meal was Middle Eastern vegetarian—falafel, gazpacho, hummus, pita bread, tabouli, lemon sauce, and vegetable sticks. The conversation was somewhat giddy and stilted, related mainly to the foreign nature of the food: "What are those little balls?" and, "I guess I'll have some of that white stuff." A nurse, a chiropractor, a teacher, an osteopathic doctor, a nondescript, pale man, and several others made up the dinner party. Black was talking, but so softly I could not hear him. He was drinking some brownish-gray liquid that looked like whole wheat flour and water but could have been anything.

Suddenly from out of nowhere boomed a loud voice: "ARMS OFF THE TABLE. ARMS OFF THE TABLE." Everyone looked to see where the voice was coming from and who had their arms on the table. The voice was coming from tiny Oliver Black, and the man he was shouting at was seated next to me. The man didn't have his arms on the table, only his wrists. He moved them anyway, and everyone went back to eating as before.

The focus of attention had now shifted dramatically to Oliver Black and everyone on each side of the table was as stiff and nervous as reprimanded children. Black's voice now could be heard, because no one else was talking. He gestured to some wrinkled gold curtains hanging in the window and said to the woman next to him, "How do you like our curtains?" Everyone turned to look. "A donation," he said. "Said the wrinkles would just 'pop out.'" He laughed, and said again, "Pop out."

We were near the end of the meal now and a man from Kenya who was seated next to me said under his breath, "Are you through eating?" When I nodded, he said, "Then put your silverware like mine." I saw that everyone uniformly had their eating utensils lined up neatly in the center of their plates. I did likewise and my plate was removed.

Apple cake was served for dessert. Black looked pleased and said, "Now if we only had some maple syrup to go with this, we'd be all set." In a moment, a plastic squeeze bear of maple syrup was brought to him; he laughed and poured a great deal on his cake.

The meditation after dinner was held in a lodge that reminded me of one I was in once at YMCA camp. The floors were wooden and dark and uneven. A large fieldstone fireplace took up one wall. A large, romantic, dark oil painting of an Indian brave occupied a prominent spot next to the doorway. I was told Oliver Black had painted it when he was young. About thirty people were in the room. Black sat cross-legged in a gold tweed chair. A lace doily, a glass of water, and some pills or vitamins were on a small table in front of him.

For about an hour, there was alternately silence and singing while two earnest young girls with long hair and bad complexions led songs and accompanied themselves on the harmonium. It was not unpleasant to sit there, and I had time to wonder about yoga and what had brought all these people to this river's edge. A book at home on yoga had said it was one of the principal systems of salvation in Hinduism and was a discipline for the realization of God through direct experience.

A friend had suggested one night that it was the threat of nuclear holocaust that made people want to find something beyond the here and now. My mind wandered the way it always used to in church. What relationship did what Black was doing have to Hinduism in India?

I looked at Black as he sat meditating: how had he made the transition from being an entrepreneur to being a follower of Yogananda? Maybe he had seen America was changing and the need in the future wouldn't be for car parts, but for new religions. Maybe he was on the cutting edge of this new trend just as he'd been on the cutting edge of an earlier one.

Certainly the Judeo-Christian heritage Oliver Black had grown up with, and which I had grown up with, wasn't offering people what it once had. What I saw with all of this was that the practice of yoga, the pilgrimages that many people had made in the sixties to study Hinduism in India, the interest in Buddhism pioneered by Gary Snyder and many others, the fascination with Native American religious ideas and practices, would sooner or later become a part of the American culture.

Despite the vocalness of the religious Right and the doctrinaire narrowness of the born-again Christians on the surface of the American culture, what I saw was that underneath that thin surface, we were experiencing a tremendously *expanded* religious awareness and an increasingly diverse religious population. Like a big river, the surface was calm, but underneath there were varying depths and many strong currents.

After the meditation, a woman asked for written questions. While people were preparing their questions, video equipment was assembled. I learned they taped every session for posterity. Bright lights and cameras were trained on Black. Two women were busy arranging his hair, his carnation, pushing his pills and water under his chair and out of sight.

Throughout the question-and-answer period that followed, Black digressed from time to time to talk about other things, most of them having to do with money, financial security, and building and expanding the land and facilities at Golden Lotus. I couldn't tell anything about Hinduism from listening to him talk, or about yoga either, but then, anyone walking into a

Christian church might be hard put to know anything about Christianity or Christ from sitting through a sermon.

"Debt is a terrible thing," he said. He repeated this several times. He said, "There is no reason for debt." He said people should "stay out of debt and be happy." He was emphatic when he spoke, not frail.

"The property to the south of us," he was saying as members of our group began signaling each other that it was time to leave and drive back across the state, "might come available. I've talked to my attorney about acquiring it. If that comes available, people could come up and build houses."

Mr. Black was at once patriarchal and sweet when he asked, "Do you like that idea? Of buying the land to the south of us? Then we could have a little colony." He was an old lion, still concerned for the well-being of his pride.

The question-and-answer period went on for about an hour with questions like: "How can I stop worrying?" "How do I know whether or not it's time to move to the ranch?" "Why is there so much suffering in the world?" "How can I contemplate nonattachment while living in the material world?" "If one has a bad habit, like smoking, can Kriya yoga help you advance in self-evolution?"

I had been ready to go for an hour by the time our group finally mobilized. We had a three-hour drive ahead of us before we could get home to sleep and I had to work the next day. The session seemed to be breaking up and we made our way out of the old lodge just minutes ahead of the majority of the people.

We didn't talk on the way down to our car. The sound of the Pigeon River going over the dam was pleasant, and the night was wonderfully clear. There were many stars.

I wanted *this,* I thought, this clarity and reality of nature. I was glad for this growing religious diversity in America, but leaderships and discipleships, in whatever guise they came in, were for someone else and religious groups or political groups—sometimes they seemed to overlap—would always seem to me like being indoors on a nice day.

Utopia on North Fox Island

Somewhere there's a black cat named Utopia. That's about all that's left of Mark Conner's dream to put a utopian community for millionaires on North Fox Island. Whatever he builds there now, if anything, is unlikely to be what he originally envisioned and planned.

The first time I met Mark Conner to talk to him was on a sunny, slushy, 22 January 1990 at Schelde's restaurant on U.S. 31 North near Giantway Plaza. (Hang on, we'll get to the black cat eventually.) He was flying in from St. Louis and I was waiting to meet him for lunch in Traverse City.

The only thing I knew about Mark Conner, other than what I could surmise from having seen him sitting in the township planning meetings, was that he was the only person I had ever known—outside of Shirley MacLaine playing the neurotic Aurora in the movie *Terms of Endearment*—who had ever interrupted me mid-phone call. When Conner had had the operator tap into my phone conversation a few days earlier to tell me he'd meet me for lunch, my first thought, before I had known who it was, was that my mother had died.

Sitting in Schelde's, a dark, generic restaurant on a muddy, salty U.S. 31 North, I am recalling Mark Conner from the township zoning meetings. Bearded and thick boned, a wearer of heavy khaki pants, red suspenders, and real leather work shoes, he was like a self-made man of an earlier generation, a young Andrew Carnegie, or a factory owner out of a Theodore Dreiser novel.

As for Conner's plan to "do" a whole island, it didn't take a real estate genius to see that islands were the next market. Fisher Island Resort, a half of a mile off Miami, was selling condominiums for more than the cost of the whole of North Fox Island, even in 1990. In 1992, according to the marketing representatives at Fisher Island Resort, the condominiums were starting at $700,000 and going for as much as $5 million.

Seaside, Florida, according to a 1988 *Atlantic Monthly,* is able to sell ordinary Victorian homes for four times what homes in surrounding neighborhoods sell for because the small streets and the ambience of white picket fences and porches makes the planned residential community attractive.

North Fox Island, where Conner wants to put up 642 homes and condominiums, has almost nothing on it. The island had been offered for sale to both the federal and state governments so it could be added to the public trust—it could have easily become part of the Sleeping Bear Dunes National Lakeshore which already contained two nearby islands, North and South Manitou—but both governmental entities declined to purchase it and it has remained in private ownership.

Islands often have strange histories and North Fox is no exception. In April of 1977 the *Traverse City Record-Eagle* ran a story stating that photographs discovered in an investigation of a nationwide pornography ring had been purportedly taken on North Fox Island at a euphemistically termed "boys camp." The owner of the island at that time, Detroit millionaire Francis D. Sheldon, who bought the island in 1960 for $20,000, was reported to have fled the country in 1977 to avoid prosecution on charges of child molestation.

Then the next anyone heard about North Fox was when Bill Walter of Frankfort was said to have purchased it for about half a million in 1987. Conner, according to township officials, had an option to buy it at the point that he began proposing his one hundred million dollar island plan. In the fall of 1989 Conner approached the Leelanau Township Planning Commission to change the zoning of the island to allow for more homes and buildings. Conner's plan called for a man-made harbor to be dug, a marina, an expanded airstrip, condominiums, a town, and an eighteen-hole golf course.

A recipient of the 1986 *Esquire* magazine's Register of Men and Women under Forty Who Are Changing the Nation award, Conner was, according to his own promotional information, "lauded for his work in St. Louis, Missouri, where he led revitalization, restoration and rehabilitation of 4 inner-city neighborhoods."

The promotional booklet is heavy card stock with the homey flecks in it of recycled paper or real vanilla ice cream. Prospective buyers are told that, "Our team Ph.D. ecologists and biologists have carefully studied the island. . . . Dunes and wetland areas will be preserved." One imagines that prospective buyers are likely to be well-to-do members of the Sierra Club or the Nature Conservancy, or have friends who are. They will need to feel that they are being environmentally correct as they buy and build homes on North Fox Island and park their yachts in the island's man-made marina, recognizing, as does the developer, that "the scarcity of marina slips on Lake Michigan is acute."

The logo is a blue-green and dark green scalloped rectangle that looks like something you'd see on a 1940s roadside diner placemat and it says, "North FOX Island." Inside are soft, artistically rendered watercolors showing what the final island development will look like in fifteen years, with the golf course on the shore and a sail boat skimming the waters of Lake Michigan. North Fox Island is described as an "unspoiled gem" and later pages say how the eighteen-hole golf course "will transform the island, sculpting it."

How can this unspoiled gem be sculpted without spoiling it? This question, in some form, is the one I want to ask Mark Conner when he arrives, but he seems tense, rushed, and so I begin more cautiously, telling him I like the logo on the cover, commiserating with him over the endless hours he's spent in attending township meetings, and asking him what he will do if he invests a lot of time and money trying to get the island rezoned and is turned down.

"Three years ago," he says, "there was a Supreme Court decision that came down that if any municipality wanted to do something with a piece of land, they had to compensate the developer for it."

Somehow this doesn't add up and I tell him so: he would sue the township if they don't rezone the land? I can understand that he would have grounds to sue them if they refuse to let him develop it within present zoning, but he's asking for rezoning.

He says it's complicated.

I mention where it says in his booklet that there are 280,000 millionaires in the midwest who are prospective buyers of homes on North Fox Island and ask if that's a large enough pool from which to draw buyers. Conner says, without answering the question, "I've been criticized for doing a utopian community for the very wealthy, but who better to do it for than people who can afford it?"

Conner owns his own plane, as well as a home in St. Louis (which he will later sell) and a second home on nearby Beaver Island, but he says he himself is not a man of wealth. "I'm just a guy with an idea. I take my valise and go and try to convince people. For the last decade of my life I've had an enormous amount of publicity. I don't want any more publicity for myself. I'm not that important."

I sense that he is going to be very guarded with me. I begin to circle the outer edges of a conversation with him, picking my way gingerly toward areas I hope he might regard as safe. I ask him if he is an entrepreneur and he says he is.

He defines entrepreneurs. "They're genuinely men who don't care about making money. They're driven to prove themselves. They're acutely aware of their surroundings."

We explore this a little. Conner says he never studied anything in school unless he wanted to. "If I took six classes and four of them were duds, I only studied for the two good ones." He attended Washington University in St. Louis, working on ore boats to put himself through, it says in his promotional material, but now he says he stopped attending before he received a degree. "I didn't study business or medicine or law. I read for three years. I've seen the dregs." He says, in a non sequitur, "I've seen rock bottom."

Conner talks rapid-fire, punctuating his remarks with glances at his watch. He takes a scattergun approach, lacing his conversation with obscure historical data, references to philosophy, throwing out several ideas at a time, making it hard for me to pursue any single one of them. For the most part, I just take notes.

Conner says his father died when he was thirteen and his mother worked as a secretary for George Washington University in order to support her children. "Once in school," Conner says, "they were collecting money for poor people. They thought we were poor. But we didn't accept their charity."

There have been other island developments, he says, Gasparilla Sound, Pine Island, Usseppa Island. Usseppa Island? "Usseppa Island," he says. "It's a bastardization of Josepha. The pirate Gaspar went and kidnapped her and took her to this island. She wouldn't submit to his advances, so he beheaded her."

Conner, a self-described nesophiliac or island lover, says he had first noticed the beautiful, uninhabited North Fox when he was working on ore boats in Lake Michigan during college, and later, when he flew over it on his way to his Beaver Island summer home. "When the mainland is selling for four thousand dollars a waterfront foot, then island development becomes the next step. This has been done on the West Coast, the Southeast, the Caribbean. This is the only opportunity to do it in the Midwest. I'm risking everything."

I pick up the brochure and tell Conner again how nice it is. I tell him that islands hold a special fascination for people and that my own father timbered-off South Manitou and nearly went broke feeding the men and hauling the logs back across the lake. I then ask him, if the island is an "unspoiled gem," in the words of his brochure, in its present state, how does he plan to, as the brochure said, "sculpt" it without affecting that.

Conner tells me I have just demonstrated something from Bertrand Russell's *Principia Mathematica* and Wittgenstein's

Philosophical Investigations but when I ask him to explain he refers to Thomas More, the fifteenth-century English philosopher and theologian who coined the word *utopia* and wrote a book by that title. "We're trying to do something spiritual," Conner says. "Have you ever been to a monastery? Monks are trained to treat everyone as if they're Jesus Christ. We want to do that with North Fox Island. I can't impress you enough with that concept and that thought."

When I get home I look up Sir Thomas More in the *Encyclopedia Britannica*. It says More was lord chancellor of England and in 1535 was beheaded as a traitor when he refused to recognize King Henry VIII's superiority over the pope. More was concerned about the destruction of the old farming communities and the increasing number of poor and displaced persons. He wanted "to restore the old villages that had been ruined by the expansion of sheep raising and to forestall the spread of the market [economy] that allowed the rich men to buy up all."

I am impressed by Mark Conner's energy and vision. It takes intelligence and hard work to put a development together. But his misconstruing the idea behind Thomas More's utopia disturbs me. Doesn't he know I can look things up in the encyclopedia? Doesn't he know that *he* can?

Even taking it all in good faith—his talk of a spiritual island development, his showy environmentalism—these things reminded me, uncomfortably, of the real estate ads to sell land in Michigan in the 1830s, which Carolyn Kirkland, whose husband had talked her into moving from New York to Michigan, wrote about in a book called, *A New Home—Who'll Follow*.

When lots were to be sold the whole fair dream was splendidly emblazoned on a sheet of super-royal size. Things which only floated before the mind's eye of the most sanguine were portrayed with bewitching minuteness for the delectation of the ordinary observer. Majestic steamers plied their paddles to and fro upon the river, ladies crowding their decks and streamers floating on the wind. Sloops dotted the harbors, while noble ships were seen in the offing. Mills, factories and lighthouses—canals and railroads and bridges, all took their appropriate positions. Then came the advertisements, choicely worded and carefully vague, never setting forth any thing which might not come true at some time or other, yet leaving the buyer without excuse if he chose to be taken in.

I kept up with the island issue for a while. I attended township planning meetings from time to time and sometimes would see Mark Conner sitting there, sometimes with his consultant, Glen Goff, and sometimes with his attorney, Jim Stevens. None of the men talked to me and I didn't try to talk to them.

I continued to admire Mark Conner's fortitude as he sat through meetings that were excruciatingly boring. They moved at a snail's pace. They addressed minutiae and extraneous matters in infinite detail, with unending unrelated digressions. The township meetings represented the democratic process at its most grindingly slow, at its most dimly and obscurely purposeful. Surely he was an impatient man—no one else I know has ever tapped into a phone call of mine—and I suspected it must have taken fantastic patience for him, as it did for me, to sit in those meetings.

I probably liked Conner better than he liked me. I saw how a writer and a developer are similar and he probably didn't. A writer wants, at the cost of nearly everything else, to see how things will turn out. A developer wants, also at the cost of nearly everything else, to get his project built. These wants put us both in those boring meetings for endless hours, and gave us a certain paradoxical camaraderie in my mind. I could identify, if not with this particular vision, at least with his having one, with his intensity, his conviction, and with his willingness to go broke if necessary trying to make his vision materialize.

But after attending a number of meetings, I decided there wasn't much new that was going to happen there. It looked like, all other things being equal, Conner's rezoning request would be approved by the township planning commission. Most of the people on the township planning commission in the late fall of 1989 appeared to be in favor of development generally.

Ron Kalchik, an excavator on the commission, spoke in favor of development and his relative Elmer Kalchik, a farmer, spoke in favor of development, as did Richard Hammersley, a builder, and then president of the township planning commission.

Still, it was not final. There were ways yet for the project to become derailed. The public at large had not endorsed the project and had not yet had their say. The configuration of members on the township planning commission could change with new vacancies, appointments, and elections. Sometimes people in the township meeting room audience were opposed to the development of the island and came and, for the most part, silently witnessed the township meetings.

At one point, John Brabenec, a sixty-some-year-old Northport organic farmer who had patterned his life after New England's iconoclastic Scott Nearing, wrote a letter against the rezoning and development of the island. At the 28 February 1990 meeting, Brabenec was present while planning commission members responded to his letter. Commission members were largely not in agreement with Brabenec.

Chairman Hammersley who spoke last, said, "It's a difficult problem and it always will be debated. I think the operative word here is *debate*. This board has never done anything that will line anybody's pockets or done anything that involves any impropriety. When we took the master plan to the first public hearing, the first volley was an attack on Gordon's [Gordon Hayward, planning and zoning consultant] credentials. We don't debate the issues. We debate someone's credentials."

Brabenec, a thin, slightly stooped, darkly tanned, deeply wrinkled man who to me looked uncannily like the two-thousand-year-old Scandinavian Tollund Mosa bog man they found preserved indefinitely in peat moss, wanted to defend himself and the contents of his letter against these last charges and say (he later told me when I asked him) that he had nothing against Gordon Hayward but was only opposed to the project on environmental grounds. Nonetheless, that evening, he was told by Hammersley that he would not be allowed to speak.

"Mr. Chairman," Brabenec said. "You said the key word was *debate,* but the very thing you said you wanted to happen, you have just precluded from happening by not allowing dialogue to take place at your meeting."

"You will have your chance to answer at the next meeting," Hammersley said.

"Yes," Brabenec said, "but a true debate would take place at the same time."

"We've had many of them," Hammersley intoned heavily. "We will move on now to the next order of business."

Earlier in the day at the Holiday gas station, I had gotten some Wrigley's Doublemint gum at the checkout counter—five packs for a dollar—and now I unwrapped several sticks and put them into my mouth and chewed. Then those wore out and so I took out that first wad and replaced it with three or four fresh sticks of gum. I just kept doing this, but wasn't aware of what I was doing.

Then I got up to get some coffee. A couple of people glanced over, and then glanced away. Conner looked over and then glanced away, embarrassed, I thought. I looked back and saw I had an array of little green paper wrappers and little silver tinfoil wrappers all around my folding chair and that's when I realized I had chewed through all five packs. I sat down and began picking up the gum wrappers. Only days later did I realize it had upset me to see Hammersley use his position to silence Brabenec and I had unconsciously chewed the gum to relieve the tension caused by my clenched teeth.

I didn't go to a township meeting for a long time after that, but when I did occasionally go up and sit in on a meeting, it looked like the process was making its slow, inexorable way toward rezoning approval. One day in August of 1990 when I called the township offices I learned that Conner was flying all the members of the township planning commission over to North Fox Island.

I had never seen the island—it is privately owned and anyone who wants to see it would be trespassing—and so asked if I could go with them. I was told there was no room on the plane

but that Conner would see me when he got back about 4 P.M.
11 September at the Woolsey Airport near Northport.

Glen Goff, Conner's environmental consultant, would be
with him, Conner said. My daughter Gaia and Berrien Thorn,
a photographer, would be with me, I told him. Gaia would be
with me because I would pick her up when her school got out
in Leland, on my way up the peninsula.

September 11 was a pretty day and at three-thirty in the
afternoon, the glowing colors of the red twig dogwood in the
swamps and the purple fescue growing along the highway in
the autumn sunlight were lovely. We took the shore road from
Leland, up and over reddish-purple hills, with the teal blue-
green waters of Lake Michigan in the distance.

The Woolsey Airport is a small cobblestone airport that
looked very strange and wonderful on this particular September
afternoon, like a big sandcastle, in the middle of a flat, golden
lakeshore pasture. We met Conner and Goff and then caravaned
back to Northport.

Both men seemed to be in good spirits as we went into the
newly white-painted Stubb's bar and restaurant. This bar had
been a typical small town bar: dark, no food, no overhead,
serious about the business at hand which had been drinking.
Now it was "under new ownership" and suddenly it was a
nineties bar, upscale, with a menu and ferns.

Goff, a tall man with cowboy sideburns, folded himself into
a tiny bistro chair. This was the first time I'd met Goff to talk
to him. We all ordered coffee, except for Gaia, who wanted a
Coke and then asked for quarters for the pinball machine. I
gave her some quarters and got out my notebook and asked the
two men how the visit to the island had gone.

"I've been a professional ecologist all my professional life,"
Goff said. "Humankind has to learn to live in harmony with the
environment, because it's a matter of survival and maintaining
the ecosystem. In order to maintain the integrity of the environment, you have to have large, undisturbed spaces and people far
from them."

I nodded and took notes.

Conner said, "Our idea is that we can have cohabitation."

Goff said, "In saving endangered species, we have thought about how to save and protect the plants. We will build a fence around the endangered species." He mentioned two—the calypso bulbosa and the lady's slipper. "The revised master plan provides for approximately two acres [around each plant]."

Conner said, "You need environmental education. You can reroute people."

Goff said, "Dr. Warren Stoudamire, at the University of Akron, is an expert on orchids. [These] orchids are propagated by bumblebees. They try to copulate with the orchids. But there are no bumblebees on North Fox now. So Warren went with tweezers and personally pollinated these orchids."

Stoudamire, I would later learn when I called Akron, went at the height of the mosquito season in May to tweezer pollinate the rare calypso orchids. Stoudamire seemed to want to distance himself from the project. "They *hired* me to come up," he said. "I know nothing about their project."

The picture of Stoudamire on the remote, uninhabited, sandy North Fox Island during the rainy mosquito season, down on his hands and knees, tweezers in hand, pollinating the petite calypso bulbosa, presents a ribald and bizarre picture, like something from *Blazing Saddles,* but Goff and Conner seemed oblivious to this.

"I'm a devout Christian," Goff said, "and I wouldn't support this project if I didn't believe in it. We want to embrace the environment in a new and very special way. We have an opportunity to approach the way humankind lives on the planet in a way that is new and spiritually uplifting."

Conner said, "I don't think it's spiritually uplifting to sit here and listen to cars go by. I do think it's spiritually uplifting to ride a bicycle."

I asked him what provisions had been made for medical services, schools, the education of the children of the people who work there, and how would those services be provided and funded in the winter, when the owners of the million-dollar estates were away.

Conner seemed taken aback, and almost instantly his mood turned belligerent. "I thought we were here to address ecology," he said. "No one wants to know this other stuff."

After a tense moment or two, Berrien said, "I think she's just asking."

Conner regrouped. "There will be no school," he said, "because we won't hire people who have school-age children."

What about medical services, I wanted to know, a hospital.

"This is still in the planning stages," he said and looked at his watch.

I asked if he thought that the island development would be at risk, in terms of being a utopia, because it would create a built-in class system. This would be unavoidable, it seemed to me, given the inherent disparity between those who would own estates on North Fox Island and those who would work for them.

"About a month ago," Conner said, "my wife, and our two daughters, and I were having dinner on Beaver Island. And a young man was waiting on us, a college student, and we had a very interesting conversation. There was no class problem. These will be college-age people working there, the sons and daughters of the people who live there."

I did not have the temerity to point out to him that he hadn't answered my question or that I couldn't imagine in my wildest dreams that the sons and daughters of the millionaires would want to work for minimum wage, or want to wait on tables or shag golf balls, or want to do it to enhance their parents' recreation and leisure while simultaneously limiting their own.

Instead, I asked him what his philosophy of life was. "My philosophy of life?" Conner echoed rhetorically, "There's only one real reason to be here and that's to create and if you can make a little money, and do that well, [that] is the most important thing. My interest is not in making a lot of money and returning to the Caribbean."

We parted then and I thought, *He has not thought this through socially, philosophically, logistically, financially, or, to use his word, spiritually.*

On the way home Berrien asked if we could stop by to visit a family where he'd heard they had free kittens. We stopped and he selected a scrawny, six-week-old black cat which he said he was rescuing from certain euthanasia because no one else would have been likely to choose it. When we got back in the car Gaia asked him what he was going to call it. "Utopia," he said after a minute. "Utopes, for short."

Time went by and it was a little more than a year later, in mid-September 1991, that I was on Beaver Island, where Conner now had his permanent residence and office.

I called from the Beaver Island dock and asked if I could visit him. His office was so close to the ferry launch that he said he could come out his back door and wave to me and I could see him from the pay telephone, which he proceeded to do and so did I. Conner looked down home and welcoming, waving to me from two blocks away, and so I was unprepared for the diatribe on the pernicious socialism in Michigan that Conner treated me to when I was seated in his office moments later.

"Other states don't have this [attitude]," he said. He railed against the no-growth proponents on Beaver Island, where he and his wife now live on Beaver Island's Lake Geneserath.

I didn't take notes. I told him I would get back to him later the next day, but the next day the wind came up and I decided to get back to the mainland before a storm hit. The radio said it might be a big one, which had the potential of keeping me on the island for days, and so I flew back to the little Charlevoix airport.

Several people had suggested that the nearly two-year process of waiting for the township to decide on the North Fox rezoning must be creating financial problems for Conner and few were surprised when the *Traverse City Record-Eagle* reported on 12 December 1991 that Conner had left a "labyrinth of legal and financial problems" back in St. Louis.

An estimated two hundred people turned out for a public hearing at 1 P.M. two days later in the Northport Public School gymnasium. Northport is a picturesque lakeshore village; even in winter the town looked quaint and inviting. The school on

Wing Street sits on a hill overlooking the village and Lake Michigan. The people all filed in and took their places in the backless, uncomfortable bleachers and the rows of rattly folding chairs set out on the basketball court, between the foul line and the basketball hoops.

This was an amazing number of people to show up on the next to last Saturday before Christmas. Here were housewives with babies, construction workers still in their work clothes, businessmen in Saturday garb, spokesmen from environmental organizations wearing suits, writers, artists, grocery clerks, farmers, lawyers, bankers, and retirees. The people at a New England town meeting in 1700 couldn't have looked that much different, other than for the way they were dressed, than the people in the school gym that afternoon.

Paul Nine, the owner–developer of the Grand Traverse Resort and a member of what Conner referred to as "the Fox Island development team," was the first person to speak. He stated up front that "because of some articles in the *Record-Eagle,* Mark [Conner] asked me to come." I had never seen Nine at any public meeting on the North Fox issue. Everyone was awestruck that he was there.

"*Mr. Nine,*" my daughter said, "isn't that the name of the ninth suitor of Mrs. Fox in the story you used to read to me?" I nodded, and the public hearing began.

"We have an incredible amount of confidence in Mark," Nine said. "We have spent our time, our money, our energy. I spent $374 to come up here on Northwest Airlines." He referred to the recent newspaper article about the financial problems stemming from the St. Louis project and offered an explanation. "That was a rehab project. That was affordable housing. And when Reagan came in he eliminated the block grants."

Nine addressed the environmental issues, saying that their clients were educated people who would want to live "fully involved with the environment" and that the housing planned for North Fox would be very low density. "We're proposing 642 units on 832 acres—that's about one unit per one and a quarter acres. Remember, these units have to support the infrastructure. If you want a good development, that is quality, you have to work with the economics of the project." Nine concluded by saying, "Now I've given you my Sermon from the Mount. Thank you for your time."

T. J. Mayhew, a worker for the probate court in Leland, got up and spoke. "Even though there's real good intent on the part of the developer and he has a right to develop it," he said, "in America, we have a tradition of doing what's best for *all* the people, and I think the density should be what was done with the original zoning. I don't feel sorry for the developers' expense. That's a gamble they took. They're adults and that's a decision they made."

Bill Burmeister, a Northport businessman and member of the township zoning board, got up. "I'm on the planning commission and I voted against this project because I began to realize what kind of impact that many homes would have on the island. I can't be for a project that would really harm the island. And I didn't care too much for the housing for the employees. They were barracks, kind of like slave quarters 150 years ago."

Diana Sullivan, director of the Cedar Wildlife Rescue, got up and said, "Historically, wildlife indicators are related to human activity. The same systems that support the lives of animals, support the lives of humans." She enumerated the ways in which the development would destroy the wildlife on the island.

Christopher Grobbel, who said he had spent six years working with the Department of Natural Resources, got up. He said the chemicals on the golf course alone could destroy the island.

Ed Reinsch, president of the village of Northport, got up and said, "That island could sink and no one would know it. I'm not saying I'm cold-hearted. That man owns that island. He could go clear-cut that island right now. He could cut every tree and take every bush. If they don't develop it, someone else will. That's the history of development."

Al Bona, a retired banker, got up and spoke, "Your zoning ordinance says that you can't approve anything that will be a burden on the township. That development plan says waste must be taken off the island [and brought to the mainland's Leelanau Township]. That tells you you cannot approve of the plan."

Jim Stevens, Mark Conner's attorney, said, "When I first met Mark Conner he told me of his dream to develop this island. In all candor, I thought he was nuts, but I've been struck by how much work and research he's done."

Sue Kopka, a photographer, got up and spoke. "I think what we're dealing with here is a paradigm problem. It's a matter of conflicting philosophies. Speaking of that, I'm concerned that a man of Mr. Nine's economic background would consider in these economic/political/environmental realities, that this would be an economically feasible project." Kopka, who has a degree in environmental planning, added, "I'm familiar with the kind of people who might be able to afford to live there. They're going to want to go out for gourmet dinners. They're going to want to go out to the theater. I don't think they're going to like it very much out there, because it's going to be darned hard to get out of there. I'd like to ask Mr. Nine what he means by people on the island living fully involved with the environment. I live fully involved with the environment. I'm a 12-volter. I live off the grid. I use alternative energy sources. It works very well. But it's a lot of hard work. I don't know many people who could afford a single family dwelling on North Fox who are at all interested in living the way I live."

Al Bona got up again. "You got a hole outside of town. It was dug before the dream went bust. You had the money to dig it, but you don't have the money to fill it. Do you have the money to fix this [island project] if Humpty Dumpty falls off into the water?"

Glen Goff, Conner's environmentalist, got up and said, "I hear people taking the ark approach. They want to make war on development in the guise of protecting nature. Folks, the planet is very sick and the way to heal it is not to build an ark, but to learn how to live in harmony with nature. And we can do it on an island, because it's contained and can become a prototype for the world."

Phil Williams, a resident of the township, got up and spoke. "It's a risky development. They're doing things that haven't been done before. It's going to take awful patient money. Your cash flow for the first five to ten years is going to be deep red and you know it."

Robert Weaver, chairman of the township planning commission, said, "From my past schooling, I know our country was founded on the idea of private land ownership. As far as this island being a special place, my understanding was that the island was stripped at one time to fuel steamers."

Paul Nine got up and spoke again. He is red-faced and angry. "I have to catch a plane, but I'm interested in addressing some of the things that have been said. If financial issues are a question, everyone here knows the township wouldn't have to pay a single penny unless it decides to do so. We paid for this hearing, paid for the microphones. On the island we pay for sewage, docks, schools, roads, all the infrastructure. This will be a seasonal community, open only four to six months a year. The only thing that woman [Sue Kopka] said that was true was that no one will want to live the way she does. As for the man who wants us not to spend our money, I don't think it's any of his business if I lose money. You do have one legitimate concern, and that's if I do something to ruin the island. [And if I do that] I will go to jail."

I left the gym when Paul Nine did and ran down to the Northport grocery to send a fax. Store owner Terry Selkirk, standing there in his grocer's apron, helped me feed the paper into the machine. I told him I'd been up at the public hearing up at the school.

Terry Selkirk said, "What scares me about this project is Paul Nine. My family lived a mile and a half from the Grand Traverse Resort. How did Paul Nine get all that FHA money? Millions and millions of dollars that should have gone to hard-up families. How did he get all that money?"

Selkirk was referring to the reportedly more than $13 million in Farmers Home Administration funds that the National Bank and Trust, now defunct, loaned Nine in the 1970s. Articles in

Michigan newspapers throughout the late 1970s and 1980s puzzled over the machinations of the loaning process from the bank, the federal government, and the City of Detroit pension funds. As recently as 10 December 1990, the *Detroit Free Press* had reported that Nine's Grand Traverse Resort had been at times delinquent on interest payments on a loan of an estimated $66 million. In a *Traverse City Record-Eagle* story the same day, Nine denied the charges.

A few moments later, as I was looking for the Diet Coke, I saw Terry Selkirk in the fruit aisle, straightening bananas, and I asked him how *did* Paul Nine get that FHA money? Selkirk smiled, leaned back on his heels, and weaving back and forth, said, "No idea. No idea."

I arrived back at the hearing just as Bob Jones, co-director of the Northern Michigan Environmental Action Council, was getting up to speak. "The developer will have to bring in top soil," he said. "More plants and insects will come."

A young man who said he worked on a golf course got up and said, "Golf courses are not natural. They are the farthest thing from a natural thing. If there are gophers, you gotta get the gophers. If there are moles, you gotta get the moles. The chemicals used on a golf course are very hazardous. We have holding ponds for irrigation and none of the employees will drink the water. It's poison."

Later, in February 1992, I saw Sue Kopka at an Albrecht and Jennings showing of her photographs at Hattie's in Suttons Bay. She said, "I don't buy this idea of Conner as a visionary developer with the vision of building a utopian community for the wealthy. I think he wants to make money. Glen Goff with his talk about the ark, he scares me, with all that born-again Christian rhetoric applied to the environment. Paul Nine and his Sermon from the Mount. How did Paul Nine get that FHA money? They're the holy North Fox triumvirate. They're the last hurrah."

People were standing around with pâté and brie looking at Kopka's strange infrared photos of Alaska and I asked her what she meant by a "paradigm," by "the last hurrah."

"A paradigm is a way of seeing or a philosophy of life," Kopka said. "One paradigm is the last generation: they went through the Depression, then after the war they thought there were unlimited goods. Then there's the second paradigm, our generation, where we have different information. We see that resources are limited. What I mean by the last hurrah is that Nine and Conner are the last flourish of this 'go out and build the Roman Empire' kind of thing."

Berrien Thorn was at the opening for Kopka's photographs and when I asked him about the little kitten he'd named Utopes, he said he no longer had her because she had never become housebroken. He related that he'd ended up taking her to the Humane Society and paying to have her spayed. He said, "Maybe she'll become someone's outside cat."

In the Leelanau Township offices in Northport on Nagonaba Street in March, township planning administrator Katherine Policoro said, "The township responded January 10, 1992, and approved his [Conner's] concept with conditions. It involved less housing, less land—five hundred homes on 40 percent of the island—but the minutes say 'refer to findings' and the findings are twenty-seven pages long. Now it's in their lap. There are so many minute details that effect everything, that there's no simple answer to this."

Could Conner sue the township if he doesn't like this?

Policoro said, "Yes, but he'd have to have grounds. We can't tell him he can't use his land. He's right. But reasonable use of the land also includes preservation of the environment. We're saying he has a right to build out there as long as he meets the environmental conditions."

When I reached Al Bona, the retired banker who spoke at the public hearing, on the phone and asked him what he thought would happen to the development, he said he couldn't imagine any prudent banker or financial investor wanting to put money into North Fox. "All you have to do is look at a map and you see North Fox is closer to Charlevoix. The only thing North-port and Leelanau Township are going to get out of this island development is the garbage." Bona hypothesized that Conner could acquire all the permits for developing the island. "Then," Bona said, "with all the permits in place, the privately owned island plus the permits becomes a new commodity. Maybe he'll sell it to the Japanese."

On a sunny, windy March day in 1992, when the whole town of Northport was glittering with ice and the trees had become ice-covered wind chimes, I walked around the small, lakeshore village, going from grocery store, to bank, to township offices. Conner's comment, made publicly several days before, that there were a bunch of "socialists" up there in Leelanau opposed to his project, was still fresh in people's minds and was the talk of the town. Policoro, unsolicited, mentioned it wryly and so did the township clerk, Peggy Reinsch, who shares office space with Policoro. Across the street, a woman in the bank said, "Most of us got quite a charge out of it."

Judy Reinhardt, a former resident of St. Louis who had recently moved to Leelanau County, said she didn't know Conner, but his developments in St. Louis had been tasteful and even brave. "One of the things Mark Conner did was he did developments within the inner city. He didn't go into the inner, inner city. He was in areas where there was some development already going on. He didn't go into the destitute areas; that would have been stupid. And I'm sure the developments were profitable. But there were other people who chose to develop in easier places. And he built homes similar to the ones that had been there." But Reinhardt, like many in Leelanau County, was opposed to the development of North Fox Island. Conner himself, for all his studied rusticity, his rumpled corduroys and red suspenders, didn't seem to understand that his visionary inner city renovation didn't translate to an untouched northern island.

There was no answer at Conner's Beaver Island business number, but Paul Nine, reached in his offices in Bloomfield Hills on 12 March 1992 said, "The township has issued a ruling which basically means the project cannot be built."

I asked Nine if suing the township was a possibility being considered by the North Fox developers and he said it was. I asked on what grounds could they sue, and he said, "These are usually constitutional grounds. Abridgment of civil rights. These things are complicated, Kathleen. It's in the hands of the attorneys. Kathleen, those guidelines are insanity. They [the township] had two years of committee work in that and they aborted it at the last minute. There is no chance that we'll abandon the project. There isn't even common sense in those guidelines, Kathleen. There's only two places to go—one is the township and the other is court."

In July 1992, the North Fox Island Company filed a lawsuit against Leelanau Township, saying the township had violated the company's civil and constitutional rights to develop North Fox. Five months later, I called and talked to Ann Brow in the township offices. She said the township's lawyer for the lawsuit, Jim Young, told them that it could take a very long time for the court case to be resolved.

In December 1992 the Michigan Department of Natural Resources granted the development permits for two marinas and an airstrip. Mark Conner is quoted in the *Record-Eagle* as saying the project could go ahead with those permits and he felt that in the end "science prevailed."

In June 1993 Conner filed a quit claim deed with the Leelanau County Register of Deeds, so that ownership of North Fox Island reverted to William and Susan Walter of Frankfort, who had originally granted Conner and the North Fox Island Company a purchase option back in 1989. The weekly *Leelanau Enterprise Tribune* reported the transaction and reported that Conner said the filing did not mean he had changed his plans.

Still, it looked like the end for the development of the island to those who lived in Leelanau County and who had been following the saga.

But it may not be. North Fox could be sold to another developer. Conner could still come up with the development money. If the proposed $120 million project took the estimated fifteen years to complete, it would be done sometime in 2010, and it's hard to see that far ahead. But one can be fairly certain that whatever is there, it is unlikely to resemble *either* Thomas More's or Mark Conner's version of utopia.

CHANGING
LIGHT

My Beaver Island Grandmother

There is a book by Johann Wolfgang von Goethe called *Elective Affinities*. It is the story of how a wealthy baron falls in love with his wife's niece and the wife in turn falls in love with her husband's best friend. The term *elective affinities* refers to the way "raindrops run together in streams," one of the leading ladies says as she oversees the building of a series of grand gardens. The cover of my edition of the book shows horses gamboling in a green meadow near a village castle under a pale yellow sky.

The cover of this book, almost more than the book itself, is in my mind as I begin a rocky boat ride to Beaver Island to examine elective affinities of a different sort in the life of my great-great-grandmother, who almost became the second wife of a Mormon there.

I step onto the *Beaver Islander* ferry and clatter up the metal gangway to the top deck. After standing in the bow of the boat for a moment I realize that I have almost the whole boat to myself. After glancing up at the pilot, I turn and settle in on the gray-painted bench just under his window.

The ferry chugs, belches diesel. Below me are cars, Sears appliances, crates of milk. It is a warm day, warm in the sun. My great-great-grandmother must have taken this trip. Mary DeMary. She had dark eyes, judging from her photographs, and dark hair.

I pull the letter about this almost-marriage from my bag.

"Dear Emily," Mary begins, writing to her daughter. "At this time I address you to let you know that some things you have said to Emma is false. . . . If it is provable that polygamy is prostitution, then perhaps you can establish the idea that I did live in prostitution when I was on the Island, but if it is not provable, you cannot establish that I lived in prostitution."

As we enter Lake Michigan, the calm waters of Lake Charlevoix give way to many small whitecaps lapping the ferry. Far out in the lake are swells the size of steepled country churches. "It is vain for you to try any further to defame my character by telling that Hiram Hall and I slept together. It never was so."

The subject of sleeping together never came up, Mary tells her daughter. "There was no such thing spoken or calculated upon between Hiram and myself," she writes, "and more, he was in my room but very little at any time. In the daytime, he set a time once that he might get time before his breakfast was ready to come to my room and make some calculations about our being married."

Rising temperatures in the middle of the previous night and a rainbow that morning had already forewarned me that it might storm and now, as if out of nowhere, a cold wind blows gray clouds out of the west, threatening rain. But it is still sunny here so I wrap my rubber tarp around me and keep reading.

Hiram wanted Mary's son, George, to come and work for him and anyway, Mary writes, "my time was up at the Townsends." The enterprising Hiram told Mary that "if I would let George go and work for him, he would fix up a house for me to move into, and if we were not married, that the use of the house and what other things he furnished me might be taken as pay for George's work."

But George was out west, fighting Indians, avoiding the Civil War and prospecting for gold. So how did Mary and Hiram expect to get him back to Beaver Island?

"You would do better to not be hatching up such Ideas and then be believing them as though they were true. . . . My advice to you is to let your mind rise to more exulted ideas. . . . Cease writing to any relative as though you ought to have sympathy

from them. . . . You will lower yourself a great deal by droop-
ing and hovering over such false Ideas. . . . " She could write, I
am thinking proudly, only to be disappointed moments later
as she goes on to deliver a classic diatribe designed to create
guilt in her daughter: "Love the mother who has born you,
toiled and cared for you, nursed you from your little infancy
through health and sickness and brought you up in a manner
that you were respected when you began to be in company."

The gist of the letter was that my great-great-grandmother
did not marry Hiram Hall on Beaver Island because his first
wife, Serene, objected quietly at the last minute. Serene, aptly
named, helped prepare the nuptial feast, but "as soon as we
were all seated," my grandmother writes, "Hiram mentioned
to the one who was called to marry us that Serene wished to
speak to him alone." Afterward, the minister called Hiram and
my grandmother aside and advised them to postpone their marriage, "five, six or seven weeks."

At the time of this would-be marriage to Hiram Hall, my
grandmother was fifty-one. She had been married to Harvey
DeMary, by whom she had five children, then widowed and
married to Reuben Nichols, by whom she had two children
who died of typhoid fever. She herself had typhoid but survived. She left Reuben when he began taking in other wives.

She adds, somewhat beseechingly, "I love my children and
don't want to be deprived of any of them. I would be glad to
see you come and see me. Emily, Andrew and children all come."

Huge waves looming to the west of us approach and glissade
under the ferry, lifting the boat several feet higher. The wave
slides under us and the boat caroms slowly down like a giant
rolling pin on a mound of bread dough.

There are no letters from Emily, married to Andrew Hale
and homesteading in Spring Lake near White Cloud, and so
we don't know what Emily's objections were to the marriage.
Maybe the finer points distinguishing prostitution from polygamy escaped her. Perhaps she was a long-sleeved puritan who
thought her mother should enjoy widowhood. Perhaps she felt
a marriage should be begun in love and anything else was a

business deal. Perhaps she was a pragmatist who recognized her mother's selling herself and George into a marriage with Hall as a *bad* business deal.

I close my eyes and think about my connection to my great-great-grandmother. I soften myself until I'm an agar solution in a petri dish waiting for something to grow in me. Not much happens.

So it's back to the letters. Ancient people, ancient lives. Mary DeMary's son George went west in 1862 as soon as he was of age, "glad to be out of that pudding bag" with his mother and sister Emma, but concerned about his mother. He writes to his sister Emily, "Please be kind to her and see that she wants for nothing."

Judging from his letters George was a strong man with a sense of humor and love of adventure. He had his gun and horses stolen, but recovered the horses after a three-hundred-mile trek through the mountains. He never did get his gun back, however, and said he would have given all the horses for the gun. He wrote about friends who died in the Civil War—both in battle and in "Rebel prisons"—and friends who died fighting Indians on the plains. He fought Indians for the United States government, but survived. Later he writes from the Rockies that "Indians here are still perfectly friendly" and intermarried with the whites as they were back East when his mother was born.

"It would be difficult to describe," Tocqueville writes in 1831, "the avidity with which the American rushes forward to secure this immense booty that fortune offers. . . . Three or four thousand soldiers drive before them the wandering races of the aborigines; these are followed by the pioneers, who pierce the woods, scare off the beasts of prey, explore the courses of the inland streams. . . . They rush forward upon this immense fortune as if but a moment remained for them to make it their own."

Land was cheap for the newcomers pushing into the American wilderness, partly because they only had to kill off the already weakened and dying indigenous people to get it. But it was a daunting prospect for many of them, nonetheless. Tocqueville in the Michigan woods in 1831 talks about "a feeling of isolation and abandon greater even than that on the ocean." I've heard people describe the virgin stands of timber as like being in a cathedral, and tell of places where it was so dark under the trees they had to put lights on the wagons during the daytime.

Mary DeMary writes to Emily that she wants to sell the homestead. "I need the use of the money it will bring so I can have something of my own to make me comfortable. A timbered farm does not yield easily to any one's comfort except there is a team of horses and a great deal of hard labour put with them."

Emma, the youngest daughter of Mary DeMary, is often ill and finds frontier life lonely. Her letters describe her mother as a cheerless taskmaster, obsessive once she gets an idea and jealous of Emily's contacts or conversations with others. She writes to her sister, Emily: "I wish there would not be such a wide water to cross before we could see one another. . . . It seems awful to be scattered around the world. Dear sister only look at this awful war. O do let us love one another. It seems as though there was not only war in the nation but in families."

Mary DeMary, judging from her letters, is practical, thick-skinned, intelligent, determined, and willing to do whatever she needs to do to survive. Her motto seems to be that if life is war, which it often seemed to be, then living is winning. Her daughter Emily seemed to have had a personality and character that was like her mother's, but since Emily was better off, she had the luxury of looking down on her mother and moralizing about her mother's actions.

Emma, who wrote of war as an extension of and reflection of the family life she experienced around her, was genuinely sickened by the heartlessness of people. Although she never expressed this in such strong terms, we see her always in her letters with a kind of vertigo. From her perspective she might have seen that marriage on the frontier boiled down to nothing more than lust, breeding, and human barter cloaked in religious hypocrisy. Emma's letters indicate that she was faint at the prospects before her.

Mary DeMary moved from house to house and place to place after the Beaver Island gambit failed. She did not want to be a burden to her children, and so although she visited them, sometimes for extended periods, she tried to find some more independent living situation.

It must have been terrifying for her to reluctantly seize her last option, marriage to the wily Hiram, and then, not only have it fall through, but be accused of prostitution by her own daughter. But perhaps she was a wily schemer herself, typically American—bright, practical, optimistic—looking to her own advantage and no one else's. Did she ever ask the good-natured George how he felt about being thrown into the bargain with Hiram Hall? Did she ever wonder about Serene's feelings?

By 1868—the year my father's mother was born to Emily— Mary seems to have become disoriented, obsessed with records of baptisms, deeds to property, and lost goods. After suffering from poor health for many years, Emma died. She was buried in southern Michigan. Mary wrote Emily that she'd dreamed prophetically of a cat and a lost trunk. Many of Emma's belongings, including "a dictionary worth $10," had not turned up, and Mary wrote to Emily that she suspected the people Emma had been staying with of wrongdoing.

Mary could read and write in a day and age when few women were educated. Harvard, founded in 1636, didn't open its doors to women until 1879, and even then it only let in three full-time female students, the other twenty-four ladies being described as "special" students.

I sit up and put the letters away. The weather has turned cold and the sun shines through the cloud cover in dramatically squared, prismatic shafts of light, making the whole lake look cloudy, blue-black, wild, like what I remember as the mood of *The Creator above the Sea of Time and Space* in the series of William Blake engravings.

A cold, driving rain begins to fall and so I go back to the

cabin. It is warm inside but smells sickeningly of diesel. Through the windows I can see the lines of rain moving toward us from out of the west, like lines on a loom with the lake and the sky the frame and the boat the shuttle.

Had my great-great-grandmother been beautiful? Beautiful women are sometimes wild and free. My own grandmother at forty-five, after nine children, still had the smooth skin, clear gaze, and elegant appearance of a Vogue model. Perhaps she inherited her looks from her grandmother.

"I could be healed by the courage of continuing to live," Anais Nin once wrote while lying in her lover's arms. *I could be healed by lying in my lover's arms,* I think now, *I could be healed by my grandmother's courage of continuing to live.*

In one letter, my Beaver Island grandmother casually mentions darning a dozen pair of socks and splitting two cords of wood "afore noon." Any woman who can split two cords of wood in a morning is in better shape than any woman I know. Still, it is hard to imagine that after seven kids and a bout with typhoid, she was an irresistible stunner, Hiram Hall's wilderness Eurydice.

The *Beaver Islander* is plowing west through six-foot seas. People are vomiting, some loudly and some quietly into little buckets thoughtfully supplied for that very purpose. But in a moment we enter a long quiet harbor with green hills on either side. I see a few white buildings at the end of the harbor and think that must be the town of St. James.

I find myself dazedly following the other passengers down the boat ramps to the dock. We all seem a little dizzy and disoriented and, like a troop of dutiful schoolchildren, mill around as if waiting to be told what to do. I decide to sit for a minute on a weathered bench and collect my thoughts. I am meeting no one here—unless you count ghosts.

Although it is overcast, it is no longer raining. Nine cars come to meet the boat; they are soon gone. It's as if a big spaceship had landed in a farmer's field, picked up whoever was waiting to get on it, and left again. An awesome quietness surges back into the empty dock area after the people leave. I am here, but nobody knows it. I stay tucked in this pocket of quiet, like a stowaway in a forgotten world.

Beaver Island, over fifty square miles in size, is Lake Michigan's largest island and has the lake's best natural harbor. I get out my wrinkled, faded map where the names—the few that I can make out—range from Mormonesque Lake Genesereth, where baptisms were held, to the typically Irish Hannigan's Road.

The rain has stopped. The town stands still in the flat, opaque light of a cloudy day. St. James reminds me of towns in the 1950s. The buildings are in an old style and some are unpainted. The cars are, on the average, twenty to thirty years older than cars on the mainland.

A weather-stained, handwritten sign on an old, white clapboard, false-fronted store says, "Sorry, we're closed, maybe open next year." I get some food at McDonough's, the only grocery store that is open. A sign on the cash register says, "Please help us avoid statements by paying the first of the month."

Across from the checkout lane there's a bulletin board covered with handwritten announcements and ads. There's an announcement for a dance Saturday with Gwen and the Men at the Circle M and an announcement for an AA meeting Thursday at 8 P.M. at the Christian church. Christian church? Is there a non-Christian church? Everyone must know where these places are because no addresses are given.

Back down near the dock, I sit down in high grass with the dark, roiled water of the harbor in front of me. The grass is behind me and on each side of me. It is dry, burnished, brass-colored grass, softly swaying, with a soft sound, like ancient Inuit throat singing or lovers breathing. I must be totally hidden from view.

The town is deserted. I feel like I'm sitting in someone's house or yard when they aren't home. I might be the only stranger in town, the only one here who doesn't know where the Christian church is. I feel someone looking at me and turn

and see the biggest sea gull I've ever seen in my life, staring at me. There are more of them; the Beaver Island sea gulls are big and bold and sentient. They look at me like cats, like cats some fairy has turned from humans into cats and then into sea gulls. I decide not to feed them.

Island historian Shirley Gladish has agreed to meet me at the Mormon Print Shop Museum up on the main street at one o'clock. She gets out of her car just as I walk up the street and I follow her up the rickety porch steps and wait for her to unlock the front door, and then we go inside. After polite exchanges about our mutual acquaintances—her son's wife's sister-in-law and husband; all fine—she asks me what I'm after. I have to tell her I don't know exactly. I tell her as far as I know, my great-great-grandmother almost became the second wife of a Beaver Island Mormon, a Hiram Hall, also spelled Hyrum Hall, and that she had previously been a widow with the last name of DeMary, and briefly, perhaps, married to a Reuben, or Rheuben, Nichols.

She lifts a hand toward the ceiling. "This is his work," she says. For a minute I think she might mean "the Lord's work," but she doesn't seem to be using "His work" in the Biblical sense. I wait. " We have records on Reuben—he was a joiner. Joiners were scarce on the island. His work was in demand." Then seeing I still look puzzled she says, "The Mormons built this print shop. It's the only Mormon building still standing."

I look around me at the square logs. I'm assuming a joiner was one who joined the logs together, fitted them together. We go up narrow stairs to a low-ceilinged pioneer bedroom on the top floor of the print shop. There's a wash basin on a night-stand, a chamber pot, an old bed, ancient linens.

I am flooded with a sense of déjà vu, not so much from the artifacts around the room, as from the way the light comes through the window. I stand for a moment looking at the dust motes in the sunlight. We go back downstairs.

Shirley gets out a newspaper—a facsimile of the *Daily Northern Islander* that was printed here in the 1850s—and turns to the back under WANTS and the ad for joiners: "It is so difficult to get joiners, that several persons have been obliged to postpone building, from the impossibility of getting the work done."

Reuben, as a joiner, would have found work plentiful, she says, and adds that the Mormon community on Beaver Island was highly prosperous. They worked hard and didn't drink. James Strang, their leader and later the self-appointed "king" of Beaver Island, served two terms in the Michigan legislature, and was an excellent orator and a good organizer.

The museum has a large library and several books for sale concerning the island and the Mormons. While Shirley looks up the birth records of Mary DeMary, Reuben Nichols, and Hiram Hall, I begin skimming the literature.

The Mormon religion, according to several accounts, had its origin in 1827 in Upper New York State, near Rochester. There on the hill Cumorah the angel Moroni showed Joseph Smith, then a poor farmboy, gold tablets covered with ancient hieroglyphics. Smith translated them with the help of miraculous stones, Urim and Thummim.

Smith had witnesses with him when he found the tablets and they testified as to the authenticity of his discovery. The translated tablets, which since have disappeared, became the Mormon Bible which, among other things, established America geographically as the place of origin of at least some of the lost tribes of Israel and as a viable source of the Christian religion.

Not to be outdone, James Jesse Strang, also miraculously and also by divine revelation, also found plates, also with witnesses. Strang's plates were found with the help of the Rajah Manchou of Vorito.

One of Strang's divine revelations told him to go to Beaver Island. "I have appointed the Islands of the Great Lakes for the gathering of the Saints saith the Lord God," we find God says in *The Book of the Law of the Lord,* under Inheritances. "I have given the Islands to them for their inheritance . . . and I have appointed my servant James the anointed Shepherd of my flock, to apportion unto everyone his portion, for a perpetual inheritance."

I wander through the rooms, still shaken by the moment of déjà vu upstairs. Here are photos on the walls of Strang and his followers. Here is a portrait of his first polygamous wife, Elvira Field, dressed in a black suit and white shirt. She initially accompanied him everywhere disguised as his male secretary, Charlie Douglas. The Charlie phase lasted until she became pregnant.

Strang, who had split with Brigham Young over the issue of polygamy, calling it "an abomination," had been monogamous for fifteen years until meeting Elvira. Elvira, dressed in her male secretary guise, stares out from her photograph, even now after more than a century, like the canary that swallowed the cat. Her eyes bear an uncanny resemblance to those of the seagull I'd seen on the beach.

Shirley finds my grandmother's records. Born Mary White

in 1817 or 1818 in upstate New York, she died in Michigan's Antrim County in 1886. She married Harvey DeMary in New York's Genessee County in 1837, and nine years and five children later, Harvey died. Sometime after that she married Reuben Nichols. It's not clear when she became a Mormon.

I find myself looking at an even more bizarre picture than the one of Elvira. This one is some unknown artist's fanciful rendition of the Mormons on Beaver Island. Called *Paradise,* the painting depicts palm trees, a castle, a lagoon, and naked women lolling around gazing at James Strang, the only person in the picture wearing clothes, a suit in fact that looks remarkably like Elvira's in the photo of her during her Charlie phase.

Of course my grandmother, like the other Mormon women whose pictures line these walls, never looked anything like those nubile women in *Paradise.* Her tintype shows a beady-eyed, stone-faced, straitlaced, thin-lipped woman to whom sensuality was apparently an unconsidered, and perhaps, from the looks of these tintypes, incomprehensible concept.

Shirley, noticing me looking, says, "It boggles the mind to consider the impulse whereby they had children."

According to one historian, Mormons believed the only way a woman could get into heaven was through marriage, and therefore a man was only doing his duty by God to marry as many of them as possible. Perhaps Hiram Hall wanted to help my grandmother get into heaven, but more likely they were both more interested in getting through the winter.

I try to think what this says about America but can't. How *did* Joseph Smith carry those gold tablets down the Hill Cumorah is what I'm wondering, and what *was* Serene thinking as she prepared the nuptial feast?

One of the books, *King of Beaver Island,* by Roger Van Noord, describes Strang's coronation. Like something out of a Monty Python movie, Strang—in a woodland setting, with a wooden scepter and crown with metal stars, wearing a robe of red flannel, trimmed with white flannel with black specks—becomes king. The coronation committee had a time of it getting Strang's throne puffy enough and royal enough, so they stuffed the arms and seat with moss from the Norway pine.

Surely my great-great-grandmother must have known about the coronation, even if she wasn't there. What could she have thought of this wilderness pageantry?

Shirley Gladish comes into the room where I'm looking at the articles and photos. She has found, in addition to birth records, a printed document, *The Ministerial Labors of Reuben T. Nichol*. It is a many-paged record of his religiosity and baptizing of people. In conclusion he writes, "It has been an uphill business and seemingly hard to accomplish any good, but we flatter ourselves that in the great day of accounts there will be found at least a few souls in the Kingdom of God in consequence of our labors in these places." I don't know why my grandmother married Reuben, but I can imagine why she left him: he must have been insufferable.

I buy several books from Shirley and then she kindly offers to take me out to show me, as nearly as she can, where Hiram Hall lived. We go down one straight road, past the airport, then turn at right angles, and go down another straight road. The Mormons laid out these roads, she tells me.

We come to an overgrown field with a few old apple trees. Shirley says she thinks Hiram Hall lived in there. *Where?* "It's all overgrown now," she says, "but judging from the plat map, this is the place."

I try to picture Hiram Hall coming down to see my great-great-grandmother, before breakfast, some gentle June morning. Did they twinkle their eyes at each other? Amidst all the "calculations of being married" did Hiram's big, rough man's hand ever graze my great-great-grandmother's smaller, softer one? Did their "polarities" shift, as we say today?

It is overcast as we drive around, not cold exactly, but just a swollen, clamped down day with violet-gray air. I point to a house we pass, an old, two-story farmhouse set back in a grove of lilacs. "That's a nice house," I say, "and I see it's for sale."

Shirley says, "It's got snakes in the walls and water in the basement." This seems to be a metaphor for something but I can't think what. Finally we are back in St. James and she drops me at the McCann House.

The Runbergs, proprietors of this Beaver Island bed and breakfast, have left a note on the door telling me what room is mine and that they're gone for the afternoon. I'm relieved to have the house to myself. There are no other guests here yet. I remember the young man I met on the boat—the one who told me about the McCann House—telling me he was going to bike around the island all day; that must be where he is.

I can't process all the information I've absorbed at the museum. In my usual gluttonous fashion I read-skimmed whole vast tomes in a short period and now I'm reeling with waves of disjointed bits of lore. Strang was murdered because he made women wear bloomers. Joseph Smith was murdered in Carthage, Illinois. Strang's wife went to Voree, Wisconsin with the children after she learned about Elvira. Strang went to Voree to die after he was shot. Wealthy Smith was Strang's first true love. The American Revolution was 1776, forty-one years before my great-great-grandmother was born: her parents must have fought in it. This last fact comes rocking up like a train into the station: our tenure on this continent is so recent, I am thinking; the whole idea of democracy and the way we do it, is so new.

America, from the time the first settlers came, was a great, hot, seething, chaotic mass filled with charlatans, visionaries, courageous and brave men and women and wild, wild, wild wildness, not wilderness, but the wildness of the people who came and who immediately went to work and went to war. War and work. Work and war. I know that from my own family; both sides. That is the leitmotiv of life in America. When my daughter Lilah's Jewish grandparents were fleeing the Holocaust and considering coming to America, people said, "Oh, don't go there. They shoot each other in the streets in America. Everyone carries a gun." And we do, don't we? Still even today. I decide to take a hot bath and nap for an hour or two, falling asleep in a high yellow bedroom with large, lachrymose pines outside. I wake thinking of Wealthy Smith. She was no fool. She had become disillusioned with James during their courtship, but then still wrote to him, attached as women sometimes are to men who are no good for them, despite themselves.

In a letter quoted in the Van Noord book, Wealthy Smith questioned James Strang's motives in joining the Mormons, suspecting, knowing him as she did, that it was "for the sake of gain," or "immortalizing" his name but then says politely and somewhat disingenuously that, of course, she doesn't think he would "try to deceive" anyone. There must have been a strong sexual attraction there; it's in her language: she writes that she is "sleepy," her "candle is burning low," and she is going to fall asleep and remember "former times." They probably didn't make love together, but it probably crossed their minds. Except Wealthy doesn't sound like the type who would have ever dressed up as his male secretary, or his pet monkey.

I get into an old, blue sweatshirt dress and go down the oak staircase to the living room. Since I am only one of two guests at the McCann House I decide I can probably use their dining room table—under an immense, ornate metal ceiling—to work on during the afternoon. I bring down my books, and the books I bought from Shirley Gladish, and begin again.

In order to keep chaos at bay, in order to fight entropy, people create community. That's a given. But it takes so much work. It takes thought. It takes fairness. It takes vision. It takes energy. It takes somebody to organize it. Sometimes it takes religion to give a new community that extra push. Sometimes religion becomes contagious insanity. Visionaries and charlatans, alike, flourish in times of crisis and it's often hard to tell them apart. People had to generate the momentum to get from England to America, from the East Coast to the West Coast. How else, except with the higher purpose of religion, were they going to do it?

Still, it would have been hard to be alone on a 160-acre homestead in the middle of nowhere with the Civil War going on and no food sometimes. Relationships between settlers and indigenous tribes were always uncertain, veering wildly from marriage to murder, Thanksgiving to massacre. The monumental *fact of slavery* would have affected all relationships: if people could be bought and sold, what was the value of a human soul? How far from slavery was being an indentured servant or a second wife?

In February with the wind howling any community would begin to look good. And who could say what was right or wrong; so far from home, why not make your own rules? "You can be as crazy as you want to be," my sister told her boyfriend once, "as long as it works."

The sun is out now, but the humidity thickens and grays the light. I feel listless. This house is lovely, but sitting in someone else's house, listening to the refrigerator going on and off, makes me feel like I'm back being a baby-sitter again at fourteen.

I decide to go into the kitchen and get a glass of water. There on the refrigerator door is a child's drawing of a sea gull. It looks uncannily like a cat. It even has cat whiskers. It's obviously a Beaver Island sea gull.

I move back into the dining room. I stare for a moment out the window into the gathering afternoon shadows of the side yard. I return to my seat at the table and continue reading.

Here's a book on the Puritans and their pilgrimage to America—their leaky ships, their bad water—nothing to drink but ale. John Winthrop, the man who brought a bunch of them over, had lost his law license back in England due to political changes. He was "between options," as we say today but he rose to the occasion, taking the opportunity to establish a colony in the New World, cheering on his seasick flock with religion, telling them "we shall be as a city upon a hill—the eyes of all people shall be upon us."

Once here Winthrop feuded with Anne Hutchinson over whether or not men could be regarded as Christian by their faith in Christ alone, or if they had to perform good works in order to qualify. Anne thought the Holy Ghost resided in each person who had faith, regardless, but she was outnumbered by those who held for good deeds. This was a political as well as religious

dispute and Anne lost. She was banished from the Massachusetts colony for her "mystical" beliefs. John Winthrop remained
in power, and in 1643, when Anne was living in New Rochelle,
it was reported back to the colony that she had been brutally
butchered by Indians, divine confirmation in some quarters of
her wrongdoing.

Times were tough in Massachusetts even without Anne's
destabilizing presence. In 1645, Winthrop writes in his journal,

The wars in England kept servants from coming to us, so as those
we had could not be hired, when their times were out, but upon
unreasonable terms, and we found it very difficult to pay their wages
to their content (for money was scarce). I may upon this occasion
report a passage between one of Rowley and his servant. The master,
being forced to sell a pair of his own oxen to pay his servant his
wages, told his servant he could keep him no longer, not knowing
how to pay him the next year. The servant answered, he would serve
him for more of his cattle. "But how shall I do," said the master,
"when all of my cattle are gone?" The servant replied, "You shall then
serve me, and so you may have your cattle back."

The Beaver Island Mormons were a variation on a theme,
one of a long line of American religious sects who, with the
impetus provided by the search for spiritual freedom, set out
for the wilderness and tried to make new lives for themselves;
but in the playing out of those lives it seems it often came down
to who got to be whose servant, the geopolitical location of the
Holy Ghost, and the finer distinctions between polygamy and
prostitution.

Finally it is late afternoon. The overcast sky is turning purple
with the invisible setting sun.

I hear the front door and see the young man from the boat
ride. He tells me he is a Christian and that he is on his annual
vacation from an office somewhere in southern Michigan. He
gestures around the dining room where I'm working and says
in an awe-struck voice, "It's like a dream come true." Then he
goes upstairs.

The original Puritans came here because they didn't want to be part of the Church of England. They were separatists. But Anne Hutchinson may have been taking this a step farther. If the Spirit of God is in each person, then each person is free to make their own choices and this would include women, but if not, then God's authority still resides in the men appointed as his ministers. How did Anne Hutchinson really die? Where does the Holy Ghost reside, and how does love relate to God and how do either relate to sex between consenting adults? What about trust as a component in the ability to truly give and truly receive love? Who will take care of the children? And when do food and shelter become a sacrament?

The young man comes downstairs, all dressed up and smelling faintly of after-shave. He says he is going out to dinner at the Beaver Island Lodge. I see him almost pirouette through the large rooms in his nice suit. What dream, I am wondering as I watch him go, what dream is he dreaming?

I move into the living room and sit on the old-fashioned, hard, curve-backed sofa under the wall of Runberg family photos, hoping that if I change sitting positions I'll be able to keep going, but I soon realize I'm about done thinking about this. Even if I could read everything there was to read about the times my great-great-grandmother lived in, I can never know everything because not everything was written. One thing is certain, life on this northern Michigan island in 1869 was not easy for anybody, least of all for a woman alone, even if she could split wood.

This was not the avant-garde, some freethinkers having a tryst, a dalliance, an intellectual experiment concerning the boundaries of relationships on the Greifswald. This was not a dream come true. This was a deadly serious contest concerning who gets to be whose servant. This was gritty frontier survival of the gritty American kind.

It's midnight or later when I wake up, upstairs in the Mc-Cann House, thinking about where I am. The young man must have come home some time ago, and the Runbergs, too. I am lying in a big, double bed in a room not much bigger than the bed.

I turn so I can look into the backyard. There is the moon with a ring around it, a kind of halo or rainbow halo.

I cannot accept the notion that men and women from an earlier century didn't feel passion for each other. The same passion that drove them first out of Europe and to America, and then out of the eastern cities and into the wilderness in search of a new dream of reality, a new vision, that made them want to transcend the mundane, the merely material, would have been the same passion that made them feel a sexual spark, a magnetic attraction in the presence of a member of the opposite sex with a fantastically different or wonderfully kindred spirit.

Sex, before and besides existing in the body, exists in the soul, exists in the spirit, exists in the person. It's all in there mixed up together. You don't get one, I don't think, without the other. Marguerite Youcenar, in writing about lovemaking, talks about the body as "that red-tinged cloud, of which the lightning is the soul." Without love, of which the physical embodiment of passion is only a part, only the blood and bone house for, without the light or lightning of love or spirit, we would have nothing except the terrible darkness swallowing us all.

Some in my family would just as soon forget our great-great-grandmother and her Beaver Island episode, but I admire her. Never in all her letters did she whine—even her bout with typhoid fever is reported by someone else—and she never tried to justify what she did, for better or for worse, by saying God told her to do it in a divine revelation.

She was honest, I think, as honest as she could be. And there was dignity in her gritty survival, if only that she didn't unduly hurt others in doing it, and that she did it at all, under whatever circumstances she had to. She was my "fish or cut bait" grandmother. And for her sake, I hope some of her affinities were elective and some of her life was lived with a little lightning.

Provemont Pond

One day in mid-April the spring peepers in the pond behind our house start calling. First one, then the other, a little at a time, until the sound swells to fill the spring day. Over the years I've noticed that at different times the frogs in the pond seem to sound louder than other times. I mentioned this to my friend Lois Beardslee, a self-taught naturalist, and she said frogs are sensitive to the amount and intensity of light and their sounds, individually and collectively, change accordingly. I was reassured to learn that I hadn't been imagining it.

Now, at four o'clock on a hot spring afternoon, the totality of sound surrounds me as I walk, making the woods along the pond and along the creek ring with a piercing sound that penetrates me, blends me into it. Behind the shrill screams of the spring peepers is the soft chirring sound of the tree toads. The two sounds together, rising and falling in waves, swales, is soothing, sensual, like the aftermath of lovemaking, the rhythmic thrumming of the blood in the heart and brain.

The bullfrogs sound the oddest of all. Theirs is a double-sucking sound, the first sound like the turkey baster getting juice from the pan and the second one like the toilet plunger in the toilet. It takes a while to get used to these sounds or to like them, to miss them if they aren't there.

It is early evening and as I walk the trail, the high hills to the west above my head are backlit by the setting sun.

As I walk and my body moves up and down, the lines of

back-lit trees seem to move, too. There is a rhythm to their perceived moving that makes me feel as if I am moving faster than I am, as if I am floating up with each step, becoming momentarily weightless, the way I sometimes feel when I am dancing.

There is a flash, almost as if there was a streak of lightning in the woods, and then both dogs—Ginger, the old collie, and Crusher, the young German shepherd—are off and running to the top of the hill. Then I see pass in front of me a giant deer, leaping and almost flying up the opposite hill.

I watch the three animals hightail it up through the woods. There are no leaves on the trees. I can see the deer and the dogs clearly.

The tobacco-colored leaves under my feet are spongy with snow melt. The only things up in the woods are the spring beauties. Their baby powder scent wafts up from the ground like an invitation.

I hear a strange sound. Is that the dogs barking? Perhaps it's ducks on the pond, but it doesn't sound exactly like ducks. Perhaps it is the dogs, still chasing the deer, barking in a peculiar way in the heat of the chase, but it doesn't sound exactly like dogs.

As I approach the house and the pond near it, I see two long-necked Canada geese on the water of the pond, moving in a strange swim-dance, their long necks going in and out rhythmically, synchronized with their honking. Are they mating? Are they battling? Are they vying for territory? Are they dancing? The rhythm is like Michael Jackson doing the moon walk. The sound, although I can't remember ever hearing it before, is uncannily familiar.

I stand for a moment, afraid of startling these wild creatures, but they seem not to have even noticed me. This is their world. This is their time. Even the dogs seem to know and go sit far away, as if faintly embarrassed, or at least eclipsed, by the geese, these rhythmic honking and neck movements, this primal dance. We have no power not to be awed, dogs, much less me. I feel strangely chastened, subdued, quiet—like I sometimes do after a movie, or the way I used to after church.

I go into the house. It is cooling off rapidly outside. I make a fire in the grate. I put music on. I am more normal than is normal. I was swept up for a moment into a part of spring that is truly wild, sacred. I begin to do laundry. It's a relief, really, to contemplate the mundane, after walking in on geese in mating season.

Mackinac Island Beacon

This story begins in Bunker Hill, Illinois, in 1897, when news-paperman Wesley H. Maurer, Sr., was born, but we pick up the thread of it on Mackinac Island more than ninety years later. It is a story about what I love about this country, but it didn't necessarily start out that way.

I was prepared to find Maurer, who I'd been told was one of the grand old men of the press, too good to be true, especially after spending a day on Mackinac Island, where everything is designed to be too good to be true. I didn't much care for this false fairyland, I told myself, where everything was Cape Cod cute. The contrived reality of the horse-and-buggy bit, the In-dian names for the hotels but no Indians, a fort looming over it all, the mingled smells of fudge and horse manure, would pale on one after awhile, I thought as I parked my bags at the Iro-quois Hotel.

Yet I came away from the island, not only having a better appreciation of its natural beauty, but feeling I'd found in Mau-rer a living icon of a newspaperman. The whole experience gave me a renewed sense of American history, a renewed sense of the slowness and effectiveness of the democratic process and a better appreciation of a newspaperman's role in that process through creating awareness and educating people.

I did not talk with Wes Maurer right away, but to people who knew him. My first stop was the office of the *Town Crier* at 34 Market Street, where Maurer has run a journalism internship program for the University of Michigan since 1956. Maurer, who spent 42 years at the University of Michigan, was chairman of the journalism department there for twenty of those years and received the university's Professor Emeritus citation.

The three summer interns are Jed Boal from Washington, D.C., Kevin Vineys from San Francisco, and Sean Reavie from St. Ignace. They all have a Clark Kent–Jimmy Olson quality I can't match with a Lois Lane quality, since I'm old enough to be Superman's mom, which is exactly the way they look at me when I ask them to discuss the relationship between democracy and journalism. We move quickly on to other matters, and things improve.

The newspaper is housed in half of a quaint, white clapboard, old-Boston-style building; the other half is a gift shop. Outside, the clip-clop, clip-clop sound of horses comes through the open window; no cars are allowed on Mackinac Island. There is a constant sense of time travel here, as though we've all been moved back a century or two or are inhabiting overlapping time frames.

Down the street from the *Town Crier* is the 1817 American Fur Company building, now the town hall. Furs from as far as a thousand miles away were brought here and became the basis for what was considered the first U.S. business monopoly by John Jacob Astor. Shrewd dealings with Native Americans enabled him to amass a vast fortune in the 1800s, which he subsequently invested in New York City real estate. Around the corner from the *Town Crier* is John Jacob Astor's summer home, built in 1819, now the Grand Cottage, part of the Grand Hotel.

A full 80 percent of the island is a Michigan historical park, and the whole town looks like a movie set for a musical about the Fourth of July. When we had gotten off the ferry at noon, the other visitors to the island and I had been treated to a fife and drum core coming down from Fort Mackinac, the centerpiece of the park. The French built the fort here in 1714. The British took it from the French in 1761 and the Americans captured it in 1783. Now as we talk at the offices of the *Town Crier,* I half expect the Rockettes to come dancing out the gift shop doorway across from us.

The interns confirm Wes Maurer is indeed ninety-one, but "very lucid," Jed Boal says. Sean Reavie, who grew up in nearby St. Ignace, has known Maurer the longest because he worked during high school at the *St. Ignace News,* published by Maurer and his family. "He is the wisest, most caring man," Reavie says, "like Yoda." You may recall Yoda from the George Lucas movie, *The Empire Strikes Back;* old and wrinkled, he is yet one of the invincible Jedi, a master of the higher truths. "He cares very much about us," Kevin Vineys says.

"When we first got here about a month ago," Jed Boal says, "it was cold. The trees weren't budding. It was very empty. But now that we've started working, we actually have a lot of work." Jed is working on an article on perishable food—the expense of getting it to the island. Sean Reavie just finished a profile of this year's Lilac Queen. Crowning the Lilac Queen is an annual tradition on Mackinac Island. I ask if they do any so-called investigative journalism, of the kind that made Maurer famous.

"The Grand Hotel has all black waiters," Jed Boal says, "like something you'd find at a southern plantation. I'd like to do a story on it. But I know Maurer would never approve."

"We cover the lighter stuff. That's just the way it is," Sean Reavie says. "He is like a father to us. He is a good man."

"We sell ads for the paper," Kevin Vineys says. "That was one of the things that really frightened me, was selling ads. Because I thought, 'conflict of interests.' I'm a journalist, not an adman. But that's one of the things he wants us to learn. Supposedly when we leave here, we could own and run our own county weekly."

They tell me they also stock the metal newspaper stands on the island, going around with a small red wagon to put the newspapers in, and collect the coins. They seem rather shell-shocked by this. I ponder this myself as I leave. It seems that Maurer wants them to know that whatever they publish can affect how much money they take in—both in ads and sales. The automatic muzzle this would put on any muckraking seems obvious. They are learning what I call "bottom line ethics" in journalism, that any stand you take that goes too far beyond the values of your community can and will affect your ability to stay in business, in short, your ability to survive on the material plane.

I want to see something of the island before I talk to Maurer the next day and so I go down to the wharf and rent a bike from one of the many bike rental places and take off on the road that encircles the island. It is a warm but breezy day. If it were early morning instead of late afternoon, I think I could circle the whole island easily in a few hours.

The bicycling is not arduous because the lakeshore road is so flat, passing as it does right next to the beach and the water. I pass a natural spring where a sign warns against drinking the water—a modern development, no doubt—and then come to the famous arched rock that has been pictured on postcards of Mackinac Island since there were people to take pictures of it.

It is high on the bank above my head, a large, man-high limestone arch, the color of a wasp's nest. Several tourists are climbing the stairs to see it and then, to the amazement of myself and several others who have paused there to rest and watch the people climbing up, two girls are bringing their bicycles *down* the stairs. They have biked overland, apparently, and are taking a shortcut down the steep wooden stairway to the road.

This is the same arched rock that New Englander Margaret Fuller (also known as the Princess Ossoli, after her marriage to an Italian nobleman) saw in the summer of 1843 when she visited Mackinac Island. Then there were no stairs. She described the "steep and crumbling path" but was charmed by the landmark, which was famous even then. "The arched rock surprised me," she wrote, "much as I had heard of it, from the perfection of the arch."

She had come by steamer up the St. Clair River, had seen Native Americans for the first time outside of Detroit, and felt that she had finally reached, as she said, "The West." She didn't seem to care too much for the people traveling with her, whom she described as "almost all New Englanders [who] had brought with them, their habits of calculation, their cautious manners, their love of polemics. It grieved me," she wrote "to hear these immigrants, who were to be the fathers of the new race, all, from the old man down to the little girl, talking, not of what they should do but of what they should get in the new scene."

The "brilliant and volatile" Margaret Fuller, as John Updike has described her in an essay on Emerson, was part of the group of New England transcendalists. She was ahead of her times in her feminist views and also in visiting the Great Lakes in 1843. She was a visitor to Mackinac Island in a time when she could see Ottawa and Chippewa families camped in wigwams outside her boardinghouse window. "With the first rosy streak," she wrote, "I was out among my Indian neighbors, whose lodges honeycombed the beautiful beach."

Now the island's Native American population has been moved back from the waterfront, inland to a threadbare little village called Harrisonville. I had visited there in the heat of the day, when I had first arrived. It was more a subdivision of twenty-year-old modular homes than an actual village, and the entire place seemed to have drawn shades, as if the people who lived there were away, or asleep.

Mackinac Island is a disturbing place and a beautiful place. It was inhabited by indigenous peoples for untold centuries, and appears in Algonquin myths as their place of origin, comparable to the Christian Eden. This is where muskrat swam to the surface with a handful of mud, according to one version of this myth, and life on earth began.

Back on trails through the hills above the town, there are breathtaking views of the water that are reminiscent of views of the Pacific from Santa Barbara and views of San Francisco Bay from the hills around San Francisco and Oakland. The village and fort are swarming with tourists, but back in the hills I walk for hours without seeing anyone. I find an amazing number of wildflowers growing profusely—wild roses, daisies,

violets, trout lilies, trilliums—lining the pathways as if they'd
been planted there.

This is the island where the movie *Somewhere in Time* was
filmed. It is an island that has a rare purity in its natural beauty
combined with its own tantalizing mystical quality. From the
high hills, looking out into the water of the Straits, I think I can
see the curve of the earth on the far horizon. Seeing this makes
me sense the size of the earth and my smallness on it, makes
distance and time both collapse and expand. The light here is
faintly rosy and everything seems to shimmer, perhaps because
of the evaporation off the surrounding body of water.

Briefly that afternoon I stop and see someone Maurer said
he knew, Frank Nephew, owner of the Chippewa Hotel. Frank
Nephew tells me, over tea and while we're looking out at the
water from the front room of his hotel's restaurant, that Maurer
had once cooked a full Chinese meal for them and had grown
the bamboo shoots himself in his own greenhouse at his home
in Ann Arbor. He also tells me that Maurer, in his younger
days as a newspaperman, back in the 1920s in Ohio and Missouri had challenged the mining bosses and the Ku Klux Klan.
I later check this with Maurer and others and learn that it was
true.

Only a short ways from the town, back in the hills, there are
deep caves. I step into one, called Skull Cave, and feel such a
strange eeriness, either from my imagination running away
with me or the actual quality of the place, that I come quickly
out again, deciding this is not a place I want to explore alone.

I wonder, standing a ways down the path from the cave,
if people ever lived in these caves, and if families or soldiers
had hidden in them during times of war. War, or the threat
of it, must have been fairly constant from the 1600s to the
1800s. People killed each other in order to live here, probably
both before and after the fort went up, that much is fairly
certain.

The Revolutionary War, which had begun back east in 1775
and ended there six years later, didn't end here until after the
War of 1812, and even then there were constant skirmishes,

small attacks, incidents of ambush, arson, and killings that were called war, or murder, depending on who was doing the killing and who was the object of the killing.

The contrast between the natural beauty of the place and the sugarcoated history of violence, complete with the fort as a tourist attraction, is unnerving. I have walked through the fort twice now, as I was crossing that way, and have seen the guns and canons, carefully tended to and displayed. If children were taken to an actual war—where they could smell death and hear the screams of the dying—they would be opposed to war. But we bring them here and accustom them to the idea of war, almost as a recreation.

I watch a family—a mother, a father, and two small boys— look through the ramparts. I look at the other tourists. None of them appear to think this is a strange world to be caught living in or a strange way to enjoy oneself. One can be an American tourist wandering the fort grounds only by not thinking about it too much. Naturally, a kind of numbing sets in.

I move beyond the fort grounds and find myself back in the

hills again, and again near some cave. But this time it doesn't bother me. I feel lonelier and more tired than I have felt in a very long time, but I don't dare give in to the exhaustion I feel. I sit down and wrap my arms around me knees and rest my head on my arms. I can see the sunlight on my arm hairs and smell my skin, which smells like pineapples.

I curl up in the fetal position for a moment. If anyone saw me like this, they'd think I was sick but I think I am far back from where the other tourists are. I tell myself that I am alive, that the world is strange, yes, and this fort and the people liking it is strange, but the earth is very pretty and the sunlight through the leaves of the trees above me is lovely.

I see the red berries and bright green leaves of a wintergreen plant near my nose and I want to pick it. I feel silly lying in the fetal position and finally my desire for the wintergreen berries outweighs my desire to retreat. I sit up, pick the berries and eat them, shake myself off and stand up and start walking again.

The *Town Crier* interns have told me I shouldn't miss the Grand Hotel and have given me the name of the public relations man there, Bill Rabe, a former student of Maurer's, now in his sixties. The Grand Hotel, however, is off limits to me that night because after 6 P.M. women have to wear skirts and I'm dressed for hiking.

I walk through pines down from the Grand Hotel and finally through landscaped gardens toward the Mackinac Island Public School. Here are red geraniums in white window boxes and broad green lawns. The long, prismatic shafts of sunlight of a summer evening shine all across the playground. A young mother supervises two small toddlers, one in a red sweater and one in a blue sweater, as they play on the schoolyard swings.

The school itself is a relatively modern, rambling brick building. I look in through the small-paned windows of the library and see a display of books that includes *The Yearling* and the Sherlock Holmes series by Arthur Conan Doyle. Soft squares of amber light are reflected on the cinder blocks of the far wall of the school library.

The mood of the island this evening is sweet, surreal. Even Fort Mackinac seems innocent of its history in the languid, long-shadowed light of early evening. All the fruit trees are in bloom. The air is perfumed with the scent of lilacs. The grounds around the fort are filled with the sounds of robins calling. I sit under a blossoming apple tree and watch as two nuns in white habits, laughing like schoolgirls, take pictures of each other with the black cannon.

I finally go back down the hill to the Iroquois Hotel, where I've been given a lovely large corner room with a view of the water in one direction and a view of the town in another. It is late, but still light outside. I shower and call home and then go out and get barbecued ribs and coleslaw from the grocery store and bring them back to the room.

By ten o'clock I am in bed reading a popular book by M. Scott Peck about the stages of spiritual evolution. Through the open window I can hear the sound of the water and I feel that I am home and am lulled finally to sleep. Sometime during the night I dream that my old dog has put his big head on my pillow. I feel awake, but my body is heavy with sleep. I keep thinking I will have to let the dog out, but I keep putting it off. This is my old white wolf dog and he has wonderful big, brown, kind eyes. Resting his chin near my pillow he begins to breathe rhythmically with my breathing. It doesn't seem strange to me that the dog's head is twice as big as mine. He is breathing deeply into my nostrils and exhaling for me. I think how brown the dog's eyes are. I feel warmth flowing through me until finally a gentle, subliminal wave of peace sweeps over me. I find my eyes closing again and despite my desire to stay awake, I fall deeply asleep. In the morning I wake up and realize I am not home and the dog, which had seemed so real, was a dream dog, much larger than any real dog.

It was less a dream than an energy exchange, or rather, the dog was giving me his energy. I had never had a dream like this, but for some reason it seemed like I had, like it's nothing new.

In the early morning quiet, I run through a summer downpour to meet Bill Rabe at the Grand Hotel. We enjoy breakfast amid bouquets of purple lilacs and pink tulips. Everywhere, discreet Jamaican waiters attend the all-white clientele.

I feel like a cross between Pony-Pony Huckabuck and Scarlett O'Hara, being waited on by black servants. Our waiter is so black, he's blue-black and as inscrutable as a sphinx. His movements are deft and virtually imperceptible. I find this unnerving; it distracts me from my breakfast. A bus tour of the Daughters of Isabella, the sister organization of the Knights of Columbus, troops through, and the looks on some of their faces—trying to act natural in an unnatural setting—pretty much captures how I feel.

Remembering intern Jed Boal's desire to do a story on the Jamaican waters I ask Rabe if it doesn't seem a little odd to him to have all one color of people eating and all another color of people waiting on them. He says he's never thought about it. "It's a tradition," he says. "I suspect it's because all the good white waiters have year-round jobs. These people come here for the summer. They're on special visas. Our guests very much like being called 'Milady.'" I do not, but I do not think it would help these talented waiters or their families to lose their jobs, which they might do if a story were done on them.

As we butter our muffins, Bill Rabe says he enrolled in the U of M masters in journalism program after the Second World War when "Maurer was running the show." Rabe never finished Maurer's course at U of M because he switched majors. He adds that Maurer was viewed as a flaming radical or liberal in some quarters. "He organized a faculty union at a time when you just didn't do that."

This time it isn't raining when I go back down the hill, walking over scores of pale wet apple blossoms, transparent and inexpressibly fragile on the black tar road. I keep recalling my dream of the night before and pushing it back into the recesses of my consciousness.

I take Rabe's suggestion of a pleasant trail through a cedar woods and arrive at the offices of the *Town Crier* at 9 A.M. to meet Wes Maurer. I find him professorial, low-key, in charge. Physically, he is small and ancient as one might expect of someone in his nineties. The interns have told me they have seen a picture of Maurer when he was young and debonair in the forties, Clark Gable in a fedora, and, because he seems to grow younger as we talk or to transcend age, that is the way I see him, or remember him.

I tell him I have just had breakfast with Mr. Rabe and was surprised and somewhat discomfited to be waited on by all black waiters. It struck me as being in poor taste, a disturbing step toward bringing back to life the old days of segregation. Maurer acts as if he hasn't heard me; maybe he hasn't, I think, as then I notice the hearing aids in his ears. If he heard me, he knows I'm asking him if he's a hypocrite; if he practices what he preaches.

"These young men are getting out a weekly newspaper," Maurer says genially, explaining their preoccupied comings and goings. "They're wonderful," he tells me as he sits down. "The whole thing is new to them, an absolute shock in many ways."

Having now learned he is hard of hearing, something I would not have immediately guessed because he is soft-spoken, I shout my questions to him. I tell him I have heard him described as a liberal. I recount to him that Mr. Rabe described him as a flaming radical. He responds forcefully, "To Mr. Rabe a liberal *is* a flaming radical." Then Maurer goes on to explain in well-modulated, genteel tones, that he is "a social critic. That's what a liberal is. A liberal lives in the future. He's hoping for improvement. He's open-minded and is continually raising questions about his own positions."

He says he designed the *Town Crier* internship program to give young journalists background in running a community newspaper, from the business side as well as the news side.

"I believe the newspaper is adult education in a democracy," Maurer says, adding that, in the profession of journalism, "the newspaper needs to reflect all that man is interested in. In the profession of journalism, we need to know more than we do and be humble about what we do know."

Maurer excuses himself to read a story one of the interns has written and while he does this I think about the tours of Fort

Mackinac and the Native Americans sequestered back in Harrisonville and the Jamaican waiters at the Grand Hotel and M. Scott Peck's stages of spiritual growth. Perhaps Maurer long ago learned he is a stage four person in a stage two world and has adjusted accordingly. I am amused by this thought and it makes me more disposed to give Maurer the benefit of the doubt when he returns.

As we talk, the young men are in and out. They wear jackets and ties. They address Wesley Maurer, Sr., as "sir." His conversation with them is infused with a sense of caring about them and dedication to the work at hand. I am struck by the fact that in a society where many grandparents are in Sun City, Maurer is here. Later when I comment to Maurer that the interns call him "sir," he will say that I might have heard one or two of them call him "sir," but he says, "I am not that beholden or formal. As a matter of fact, most of the interns I have served address me as 'Wes,' a few as 'professor.' I am, thank God, addressed very rarely as 'sir.'"

Maurer's own newspaper career spans almost a century. He has received numerous awards and citations in education and journalism and in 1986, Governor Blanchard named August 8 Wesley Maurer Day. In 1924, at an early stage in his career, he edited the *Athens Messenger* in Ohio, concurrently with teaching ethics at Ohio University. Courageous newspaper articles telling the miners' side of the story, as well as that of the mine operators in the mines in nearby Hocking Valley (among them articles on mines owned by T. R. Biddle who was also a trustee of Ohio University) ultimately cost Maurer his job at both the newspaper and the school.

Fortunately for Maurer, the very things that cost him his job in Ohio made the University of Michigan want to hire him. He describes his time in the Hocking Valley as "exciting" and "traumatic," but that he learned a lot. Such a lot, in fact, that he seems to want to hold the reins on his young interns rather tightly. He must know that they chafe under his restrictions because as he talks to me, I feel it is for their benefit.

"One of the things we're trying to develop here is attitudes.

Why is the newspaperman cynical?" he asks rhetorically. "Because he doesn't know enough. He thinks people have faults. But there is another attitude. We try hard for the reporter to begin to see his humility, that he knows not enough to write about even the Mackinac Island City Council. He must study political science. But he still will not know until he gets the opportunity of seeing the city manager and city council in action. A community comes down to individuals. You come to know how people react to your writing. You come to know these people who know you as a reporter. So, if he can begin by being humble, by trying to understand the different cultures in a community, that is where we start."

Newspapers are "adult education," as Maurer says, or, to say it another way, they "bear witness," yet how does one know what to tell and what not to? When to go against the prevailing social norms and when not to? It is the compelling drive of almost every honest writer to bear witness to the times we live in, and perhaps Maurer is not actually trying to discourage his reporters from doing that, but more likely, he wants to give them a good solid grounding in the basics, and an awareness of all the dynamics involved and all the risks.

At another time, in an interview with Dr. John Tanton, Maurer will indirectly address this issue. "Enlightenment," or education, adult or otherwise, "comes slowly, in my opinion," he tells his friend Dr. Tanton. "We cannot hasten it."

Maurer in fact is far ahead of his times in believing "poverty is caused by a social policy of greed, of not sharing," but he doesn't expect people to share his view until they see that "the death of humanity" will result from this greed.

"Can man create a society that influences individual members to give their lives in cooperation so that humanity may live, not die?" he asks. And he answers his question, by saying that such a society can be created "through discipline—the discipline of accuracy, of honesty, the discipline of professions, of knowledge and of morals," and in his profession, through the professional disciplines inherent in journalism.

Maurer sees that there is wisdom in justice, and this justice—

political, racial, and economic—he sees as important to the survival of the human species, but in order for that view to prevail,
"It must be all through common consent." What Maurer seems
to be saying is that we evolve not just individually, but collectively, and newspapers can help to inform people, and thereby
educate them, but they cannot make people arrive at a point of
view before they are moved to do so. Perhaps Maurer is in fact
not lagging behind his interns in moral fortitude, but is way
out in front of them. How many of them will stand up to
mining bosses, or the equivalent, in their lifetimes? How many
of them will be nurturing the spiritual and intellectual growth
of others when they're in their nineties?

In an essay entitled, *The Newspaper in a Free Society,* a speech
that he delivered to the St. Ignace Kiwanis Club in 1975, and a
copy of which he gives me to read while he attends to his
reporters, Maurer defines the newspaper, through the words
of Dr. Fred Newton Scott, head of the University of Michigan's
Department of Rhetoric and Journalism, and Maurer's boss
when he was instructor of journalism there from 1924–25, as,
"nourisher of the human spirit, reflector of every human interest.... A good newspaper is one which co-operates with the
community to create a community bond."

This bond, Maurer goes on to say in the essay, is comprised
of "subtle and elusive qualities they are identifiable [as] a generous and continued concern for the children, the aged, the needy,
the deprived, even for the wayward." It is these qualities that a
good newspaper can foster, he writes, and that help to create
in the community "a sense of decency, of grace and of common-
weal."

The issues facing a society are not always easy to deal with;
if they were, a newspaperman's job would also be easy: where
there is no conflict there is no risk. Maurer uses the example of
the controversy surrounding the abortion issue to talk about the
process of democracy. There is a moral value attached to life,
he says, and a moral value attached to choice. "We have a
[democratic] system whereby we can learn [through] the process of experimentation; that's good science, too." And not

until all have had a good, long time to consider the issue, to submit it all to lengthy discussion, will there be a resolution. That is the democratic process and it's as useful as it is difficult.

Maurer regards the democratic process as alive, *dynamic* is his word. He sees it as a way for human beings to grow in knowledge and wisdom, to grow spiritually, individually, and collectively. He tells his friend Dr. Tanton, "I think the primary interest I have is to bring myself, as well as others, to a realization of the tentativeness of life, and of the seriousness of using it not selfishly, greedily, but as proudly as possible to better the circumstances for all of us."

Maurer believes that all people universally have a sense of right and wrong and that survival itself mandates moral behavior. "All the Ten Commandments," he says, citing the commandments against stealing and against lying as examples, "are for survival." One of the major moral requirements of human beings, he says, "is to [physically and emotionally] take care of children [because] that's the survival of the future. If they're not taken care of, they are abused, and that results in hate, and thus they engage in crimes because of their hatreds."

Maurer began his formal education as a seminarian but eventually became a newspaperman. His "deep interest in religion" still imbues his conversation and his writing and he expresses compassion for the poor, for justice toward them, "for social awareness, for the democratic concept that a society should provide security for all." Sunday mornings are the time he chooses to spend with his young interns.

Maurer's beliefs, I feel, can't be understood in narrowly journalistic terms, but have to be seen in the context of larger spiritual concerns, such as brotherly love or universal love—using here the Greek word *agape,* or in light of the notion of individual free will, or in the context of democratic freedoms generally. In fact exactly this issue came up with regard to newspaper coverage of the Ku Klux Klan when he was working in Mexico, Missouri, during the 1920s for the *Mexico Evening Ledger*. He suggested to the publisher that they write an editorial against the Klan, and his publisher said, "We aren't running a church here." Maurer responded, "I know, but there's no reason we should have a separate idea of morality just because this is a newspaper."

Honeysuckle and mock orange are blooming in the backyard behind the newspaper. I can see them through the window, as well as those peppermint-pink tulips that seem to be an island species.

"Every Sunday morning I meet with the reporters for three hours," Maurer says, "here at the *Town Crier*. I always try to bring the conversation around to attitudes. This has connections to morals, to honesty, to responsibility, to commitment, to love of the work and the profession."

It is reassuring to know there is still a place where, especially in journalism, there is something that has connections to honesty, morals, and love of the work. These are the kinds of connections I have grown fond of over the years. I recall, as Maurer talks, a cartoon that ran a while ago in the *New Yorker*. It shows the devil welcoming people to hell, saying as he does, "There's no right or wrong here, just whatever works for you."

Lately, it has sometimes seemed that this is not just a cartoon in some places, but reality, and it is good to know that somewhere, even if only in the rarified, lilac-scented atmosphere of Mackinac Island's clip-clop life, another reality exists.

I thought about Maurer often after that first visit, and in the late summer of 1991, I was able to go back and visit him. I took my youngest daughter, Gaia, with me, because I wanted her to see, in the flesh, a man who had tried to live according to his beliefs.

It is about ten in the morning, in late August when we arrive at the *St. Ignace News* offices and there he is: Wesley Maurer, Sr. All around him, his entire newspaper has converted to computers, but he has not. He chats politely with us, stands still for a few photographs, then says, "I have some copy to edit, Miss Stocking, or I would enjoy very much spending more time with you."

I was, I honestly must admit here, rather astonished to find him not only still alive, but cogent, still carrying on in his usual manner. It was uncanny, as if he was one of the immortals.

Another two years have gone by since that last visit and a Saturday morning phone call to the *St. Ignace News* finds Dick Hayden at work, and he shares the news that Wes and his wife Margaret are soon going to celebrate their Golden Wedding Anniversary at the Grand Hotel and that Maurer is still working.

In my mind, I see him as I saw him last, with those pin-striped, dark-blue old-man pants pulled up above his waist, standing at the proofing table, grease pencil in hand, patiently editing copy. And, to borrow a line from the ancient fairy tale, if he is not gone, he is there still.

Sunny Swanson's Vegetable Stand

Sunny Swanson has a farm down the road from me. It sits at the base of a large hill called Sugar Loaf Mountain.

The vegetable stand has a big scale hanging off to one side—like the kind Lady Justice has in the pictures of her—to weigh the broccoli and tomatoes, and it has old paper bags from the grocery store for the vegetables. This is a self-serve vegetable stand, and there's a dish for money and a Big Chief tablet to do your arithmetic.

Local people come here because the vegetables are good and cheap and because Sunny grows the best sweet corn in the county.

Tourists come too and I've stood there as they marvel at the vegetables and the trust that's been placed in them to make their own change.

They often seem nervous—doing their arithmetic out loud or laboriously writing down their purchase of three zucchinis, and entering sixty cents next to it—as if they think hidden cameras are watching them.

I like this vegetable stand and I like it when Sunny comes up from his fields with a load of produce and stays to talk.

The secret to good corn, he says, is to pick it fresh a couple of times a day.

Sunny is seventy-three. This was his father's farm before it was his. "When I was a kid, I worked, hoeing with my brother.

Of course we goofed off, the way kids do, the middle of the afternoon, 'we'd head for the lake. See that," he says, pointing to a bare plot of ground. "The deer took down that quarter acre of broccoli and cabbage—now I don't need to hoe it."

I ask what the deer eat most of.

"Oh, deer get different notions," he says. "They'll get hepped up on a certain thing. Then they won't eat it no more. They'll switch to something else."

In a field of squash he has sticks with white rags tied to them. I ask him what that is.

"That's Sweetheart soap," he says. "Bought a big case of it last year, paid almost fifty dollars for it. A lot of little bars in there. You tie a rag around each one and hang 'em up. Supposed to be a deer repellent. Sometimes it seems to work, sometimes it don't. The deer seem to get used to it after a while."

Sunny's season begins in February, with setting seeds in the green house. By mid-May he's working ten or twelve hours a day in his fields. He does all the work himself, he says, "that way there's no loss." He figures he'll farm for another year or two before he stops for good.

Sunny's philosophy of life and faith in people is summed up by a hand-embroidered sign at the back of the vegetable stand, which reads, "God knows everything, thank you for being honest."

Outer Space

It is a windy spring day and I am driving along a little country road deep in the Antrim Dells, the kind of Michigan back country road travelers tend to feel lost on even when they're not because of the way the road wends its way around the lacy borders of lakes. Torch Lake. Lake Bellaire. Skegemog Lake. Central Lake. Intermediate Lake. This is the kind of Michigan landscape that makes people who fly over it in a plane, amazed at the number of lakes one state can contain.

On a midweek day, it is a strangely deserted landscape pulsing with the sound of frogs calling. Only once do I see someone, at a distance: a woman pulling a child in a red wagon, small as figures in a Chinese painting.

It is hot inside the car and I roll the window down and continue driving slowly along. Mine is the only car on the road. Back from the gravel road, at an old farmhouse, I watch the April wind whip the wash on a line, wildly, first one way and then the other. Next to the car, in a drainage ditch, the water runs with the heady sound of spring snow melt. There's a flash of dazzling yellow and I glimpse a clump of marsh marigolds blooming in the swamp.

Finally there's a tower in a yard and an old brown shingle cottage. I glance again at what I'd written on the yellow legal pad on the seat beside me and see that a house and tower like this are part of the directions John Shepherd had given to me over the phone of how to get to his Project STRAT.

I pull into the driveway and get out, all the while thinking I must be in the wrong place. This lakeside cottage seems unlived in as well as being an unlikely place for a space station. I knock on the door. A line of poetry I memorized in seventh grade comes back to me: "*'Is there anybody there?' said the traveler, knocking at the moonlit door.*" Large, gray clouds are boiling up in the south, over the lake in front of the house. I'm sure I must be in the wrong place. Perhaps it is dangerous to be here, alone at a stranger's house. Although I'd heard through the local grapevine about this man's attempts to contact extraterrestrial life, no one I'd asked for directions—certainly not Twyla at the Torch Lake Gas Station and Party Store, who sold me a delicious cinnamon roll—had ever heard of John Shepherd or his Project STRAT (Strategic Telemetry Research and Tracking).

At the moment it is hard to believe he exists or, if he does, that this is the place.

But it is.

John Shepherd, when he comes to the door, looks like a cross between a scientist in a Spielberg movie and Mother Teresa and I know immediately that this is it. He has the deep-socketed, fervent eyes of a religious aesthete and the distracted air of a preoccupied scientist. He is extremely cordial, in a practiced way.

We step inside and I am in a setting that is jolting in its contrasts: the cottage board floors, the knotty pine walls, the red linoleum kitchen counter tops, the deep, double kitchen sink to my left; then, to my right, a thick, double-paned glass wall, behind which is a two-story accelerator pit, flashing lights, illuminated computer panels, and high-voltage warning signs. It is like being in a divided mind, one side a cottage from the past and the other a personal radio station from the future.

For the last fifteen years, John Shepherd says, as he politely takes my coat and hangs it up, he's been beaming signals into space from here, to try to connect with extraterrestrial life.

Meanwhile, I am reeling from the juxtaposition of the old, dark, somewhat down-at-the-heels but homey cottage on the one side, and the shiny, complex, scary-looking, spanking new, modern equipment on the other. John Shepherd's demeanor is that of a congenial tour guide, and the contrast between that surface personality and the more complex personality that one can only imagine lies beneath the surface, is also disquieting.

As if sensing my bewilderment, he says, "Well, time to change the tape," and goes over to his tape machine and, putting on a lovely piece of jazz, looks at me, as if I am directing him, or as if he is trying to please me and says, "Let's play this."

I am touched by this gesture of hospitality. And then the thought occurs to me that probably nothing I do will be too strange for him: he's used to imagining an alien in here, so his politeness skills have developed in preparation for this event.

He looks over toward the radio control room and then back at the computer terminals in the living room. "My interest in all this," he says, "started with a love of energy, a certain drive to be with it and around it. It's like a love affair. It's almost a unity thing. At certain times, I can reach this high degree of consciousness. I was always fascinated with the mystery of electricity, lightning. My interest is in finding out about the unknown, and the unknown is just that: the unknown."

He is enthusiastic about a new transmitter he's planning to get that will allow him to beam signals into space much farther than before. I am shivering and ask to put my coat back on. He gets my coat for me and says, "I'm sorry you're cold." He offers to make me hot tea and after demurring for a moment, I accept.

While he is making the tea, I walk around the living room and look again into the room with the two-story transmitter and the high-voltage warning signs.

He brings the tea out and puts it on the low table in front of the 1950s-style Danish modern sofa and invites me to sit down. I am feeling awkward, and, not wanting my host to think it's because of him, I tell him the high-voltage signs make me nervous, that once as a child, washing dishes for my mother, I accidentally had a wet copper Dolly Duz-It in my hand when I turned off a light that had a faulty electrical switch, and that shocking experience has stayed with me and that, indeed, I still have an ignorance and fear of electricity.

He graciously accepts this explanation, as if it were an everyday occurrence. He changes the subject, introducing his cat, Neutrino. "Neutrino was named for an elusive subatomic particle," he says, indicating the tabby crawling up into his lap, "but she isn't very elusive." He hands me a cup of hot tea and now, holding the warm cup in my hands, I begin to feel more at ease.

He moves photo albums on the coffee table to better situate the teapot and I learn that he was abandoned in Detroit by his natural mother after her husband abandoned her, and was raised by the mother of one of his mother's erstwhile boyfriends. He tells me he flunked kindergarten. "They'd leave the door open and I'd go down and talk to the men in the boiler room—you know, kindergarten; drawing giraffes and stacking boxes—after awhile there's just so much you can do with it." After dropping out of kindergarten, he was home schooled and a teacher came to the house twice a week. While studying on his own, he says he pursued whatever interested him and more or less "intuitively" learned electronics and physics.

He moves the photo albums again and tells me that until recently he had a roommate. He shows me photos of a tall, very strong-looking, dark-haired young man. "He was also a castout from society. He was abused, deeply abused. He liked knives. He was a Roman soldier. I was an aetherian. I had more light, but we were amazingly compatible. He was an unsettled person. Even when he was loved and cared for, he couldn't stay in one spot." His friend has recently moved to Ohio, and he misses him; he even misses the way his large friend would "thump, thump, thump" through the house, shaking everything, something he thought he would never miss.

He tells me his grandmother, Irene Lamb, the woman who raised him, is very ill, is in fact dying as we talk and so he feels a little upset and distracted himself. He is half expecting a call from the nursing home as we talk. "She is like a mom to me," he says, "real close, real caring. Always there when things go wrong. Never overbearing. Very open-minded. A true example of what Christianity is without preaching it."

The story he tells of how he was found by Mrs. Lamb, abandoned in a baby crib in a freezing Detroit apartment, is a classic tale of survival, the mysterious workings of fate and the triumph of love. The woman who was to become his mother or grandmother, he says, came in and found him cold and dirty in a crib lined with baby bottles, as if he'd been left a supply.

I mention that perhaps his name should have been Lamb and hers Shepherd and he says many people comment on their names, adding, "I think she had a profound love for me. I think she thought I had a gift—and I do, too. And she thought such a gift had a right to grow. My grandmother was the main one who encouraged me with the electronics and the radio station. My grandfather tried to keep it under control." John makes a flattening-out motion through the air with his hand, "but still encourage it."

He says he is a self-taught physics and electronics buff. "I don't really know where my knowledge came from. Sometimes I feel like I may be descended from Atlantis and it's an intuition from within. When I get a piece of information or [piece of] equipment and put it together with something else, it just comes to me."

I am half expecting to hear a Whitney Streiber–type *Communion* story, the kind where he says he was abducted by space aliens at an early age and has been trying to get back in touch with them ever since. But no, John says his interest grew slowly out of his interest in electricity and was initiated somewhat by watching Glen Larson's "Outer Limits" on TV.

In fact, he has never seen a space being, or anything close to one. He has been waiting all these years for signs of intelligent life in the universe. "It would be so exciting," he says. "It would change the course of history."

The closest he came to an unexplained event was one night in Detroit in the early 1960s. "I was standing in my backyard and I saw something unusual. I spotted a star that seemed to be moving. I went and got my 10-power spotting telescope. It was moving, like, from east to west, on a clear night, around nine o'clock. I put my back against the house and lined it up between two wires, to make sure *I* wasn't moving."

He says he knew it wasn't a plane. "It didn't appear to have the required running lights an aircraft carrier is supposed to have. It made no noise. It released a smaller object—a speck of light—which airplanes are not supposed to do over a city. The larger light continued on directly overhead and the smaller speck of light descended very gradually until it became invisible or faded into the skyline of the city. I thought, well, that's pretty unusual."

From that point on, he says his interest in outer space increased. Gradually he was able to collect the electronic equipment he needed from junk shops, yard sales, donations, and the dump. He built the space station onto his grandmother's cottage slowly over a period of time, starting in the late 1960s.

In the front of Carl Sagan's book, *Contact,* some anonymous book jacket bard writes, "For centuries humanity has dreamed of life and intelligence beyond the earth; for decades scientists have searched for it in every corner of the sky. . . . Then, one afternoon, the MESSAGE, awaited for so long, arrives. *Contact* has been made."

That's the scenario John Shepherd has been hoping for these past twenty years, but so far he's had only two modest indications of something out there that can shine, shimmy, or show up on a radar screen. Twice, both times in the fall of 1973, when there were a number of UFO sightings in the area, he says, "We picked up some interesting energy activity.

"We know less about outer space than Columbus did about the New World," he says. "The ultimate goal would be final contact. I think that would be of great benefit to man. I don't get discouraged. The desire to discover never goes away. You search and you continue searching because of that desire, and because of that, you know there's something there."

A voltage warning begins to scream and I ask him how many minutes we have before the place blows up. He says about ten and I decide to wait for him outside while he goes into the substation to fix whatever it is that's making the red light flash on and off.

The house and yard are a boy's house and yard. From ancient beds of myrtle and pachysandra emerge bits and pieces of electromagnetic equipment. In the driveway is a new red Fiat. A landscaped stone walk leads down through a garden to the lake, but it looks as if it hasn't been tended to or even used much in years.

I think about there being other people, or other kinds of life, in the universe. It's hard to imagine that there isn't something out there. Someone told me that all the TV shows have gone out into space: "Howdy Doody," "I Love Lucy," "Gomer Pyle," "The Honeymooners." I try to imagine how this might be received. My neighbor Susan said she couldn't conceive of beings in the universe dumber than we are. In which case, she said, she'd decided that we here on earth must be either a zoo or a laboratory.

John comes out at that moment, having apparently fixed whatever was causing the siren to go off, and seeing me glance at the lovely red car tells me that it has a lightning finder on it: a screen in the car shows ionization so he can go to wherever lightning might be about to strike.

I must look amazed because he says he hopes this isn't going to be "another nut" story. I tell him what Francis Bacon said, "They are ill discoverers that think there is no land, when they can see nothing but sea." I do not tell him what Seneca said: "There is no great genius without some touch of madness." But I do remind him that Ben Franklin experimented with lightning, which of course he already knew. Leonardo da Vinci, who was not like everyone else, thought he could fly if he could just get the wings right, and he came close enough that his drawings were referred to by the Wright brothers, among others; who knows, if he'd just gotten them a little bit more right, he probably could have flown off that hill in Italy. Galileo was considered a heretic because he thought the earth revolved around the sun when normal people knew it was the other way around. Alexander Graham Bell was considered a bit off by his neighbors when he was in the throes of trying to invent the telephone we all talk on.

It's me, I explain to him, not him. I am so lacking in what he calls intuition about electricity that I'm afraid, as with the wet copper Dolly Duz-It, I will unwittingly stumble into or over just the thing that will turn me to burned toast.

John relaxes then. He points out a towerlike structure in the center of the yard and tells me it is the skeleton of a new transmitter accelerator. It will allow him to beam signals ten times farther than previously. He tells me he's going to fire it up Saturday and wouldn't I like to be there? I decline, reminding him of my trepidation about lightning and firings up, but suggest that a friend of mine might love to be there and so he extends the invitation to my friend.

We move back inside so I can get my coat and he excuses himself to go into his space laboratory, where he puts on head phones. I hear him say, "Hello, this is John Shepherd. It's 10 A.M. and Project STRAT is on the air. It's a beautiful day here in northern Michigan and we're going to play a little reggae for you, some Bob Marley, some Barr Phillips. Please stay tuned for more jazz and reggae this afternoon. This is Earth Station One, coming to you from beautiful northern Michigan."

I am on my way home from his place that afternoon when it slowly starts to snow again, dusty little flakes. A wasp that had apparently, unbeknownst to me, flown into my car, perhaps when I rolled the window down that morning, crawls sleepily along the rim of the dashboard, between the dashboard and the front window of the car. Later I tell my friend Scott Murto, a graduate of the University of Michigan engineering school, about Project STRAT and the Saturday firing up, and he does go and later tells me about it.

"I walked into that house and freaked out," Scott says. "He's doing the kinds of things I always wanted to do as a kid, with flashing lights and switches. He's doing his science fiction dream. He's trying to contact UFOs. I was in grade school when we put a man on the moon and technology was 'a god' and space was the new frontier and it seemed anything was possible."

Scott's friend Jennifer Slack, who went with him that day, says, "It was amazing to me to walk into this little house in Central Lake and find a *laboratory*. Science has become institutionalized in the last century, but here's this guy in Central Lake and he's as committed, or *more* committed, than scientists in universities. This is *not* a hobby. He works eighteen hours a day. Yet he's never had to write a grant or justify his research to a committee. It's reassuring and refreshing just to find him *there*."

But what do those electronic signals really do? As Scott points out (this would not have occurred to me), this is a noisy planet and electromagnetic signals louder and longer than Shepherd's are probably going out past Mars and the moon all the time. If you were a space alien, this planet would probably sound like a giant party. How to find Shepherd in all that racket?

Jennifer says that what John Shepherd was actually trying to do was *lure* the space aliens in with the music. The music was the signal, she says. She does a quick takeoff on his radio spiel: "Hello, this is John Shepherd. It's 3 P.M. and Project STRAT is on the air. It's a beautiful day here in northern Michigan. Any of you ETs out there, please stay tuned for more music this afternoon."

If you call Shepherd in Central Lake and get the answering machine, you'll probably hear, "This is John Shepherd at Project STRAT," etc., and that you can leave a message for him, "or anyone else here at the project," which sounds like twenty NASA guys in white jumpsuits are running around, but as far as I know the only person at the project in any official capacity is John Shepherd.

What do I think of all of this? I think that if I were in a foreign place—say Mt. Everest or Namcha Barwa in the Himalayas—someplace where I imagine the weather must often be like Michigan's in April, with hot sun in the morning and snow by afternoon. And let's say I had been hitchhiking all day with one of those groups composed of people from all over the world—and late that night after we've eaten our dinner of hard cheese and unleavened bread and passed the wineskin around, when we're all sitting around the campfire—let's say somebody asks me what America is like. I would tell them about John Shepherd and his surrogate grandmother who found him in some modern-day equivalent of the bulrushes in Detroit, his Strategic Telemetry Research and Tracking Station, his friend who was like a Roman soldier, his cat Neutrino, his cottage on Intermediate Lake Drive with the space station growing out of it like a giant mushroom, the red Fiat with the lightning finder, and then I would say, before walking away from the glowing campfire and retiring for the night to my yurt, "America is like that."